Answering Back

Carol Ann Duffy was born in Glasgow in 1955. She grew up in
Stafford and then attended the University of Liverpool, where she
studied philosophy. She has written for both children and adults,
and her poetry has received many awards, including the Signal Prize
for Children's Verse, the Whitbread and Forward Prizes, and the
Lannan Award and the E. M. Forster Prize in America. In 2005, she
won the T. S. Eliot Prize for *Rapture*.

Also by Carol Ann Duffy

Standing Female Nude
Selling Manhattan
The Other Country
Mean Time
Penguin Selected Poems
The World's Wife
Feminine Gospels
New Selected Poems
Rapture

FOR CHILDREN

Meeting Midnight
Rumpelstiltskin and Other Grimm Tales
The Skipping-Rope Snake
The Oldest Girl in the World
Underwater Farmyard
Moon Zoo
Queen Munch and Queen Nibble
The Stolen Childhood
Doris the Giant
The Good Child's Guide to Rock 'n' Roll
Collected Grimm Tales
Another Night Before Christmas
Beasts and Beauties

AS EDITOR

I Wouldn't Thank You for a Valentine
Stopping for Death
Anvil New Poems
Time's Tidings
Hand in Hand
Out of Fashion
Overheard on a Saltmarsh

Answering Back

Living poets reply to the poetry of the past

edited by CAROL ANN DUFFY

PICADOR

First published 2007 by Picador

First published in paperback 2008 by Picador
an imprint of Pan Macmillan Ltd
Pan Macmillan, 20 New Wharf Road, London N1 9RR
Basingstoke and Oxford
Associated companies throughout the world
www.panmacmillan.com

ISBN 978-0-330-44824-6

9 8 7 6 5 4 3

A CIP catalogue record for this book is available from
the British Library.

Typeset by SetSystems Ltd, Saffron Walden, Essex
Printed and bound in the UK by
CPI Mackays, Chatham ME5 8TD

Visit **www.picador.com** to read more about all our books
and to buy them. You will also find features, author interviews and
news of any author events, and you can sign up for e-newsletters
so that you're always first to hear about our new releases.

For Simon Powell and Imtiaz Dharker with love

Contents

Foreword

For this anthology, *Answering Back*, I invited the best of our contemporary poets to select a poem, or poem in translation, from a poet from the past which they would like to answer in some way. Around fifty of the poets responded. The choice of each poet is printed here alongside his or her own, new, answering poem. The reason for each individual choice was entirely up to the poets: some chose to subvert or to argue, some to play or to tease, some to echo or to transform, others to pay homage or to elegize. Throughout, there is a strong sense of the living and the dead poets' belief in the triumph of language over time. As Gillian Clarke writes, 'I want to say to the dead, look what a poet sings/ to life'. Poets, as Patrick Kavanagh wrote, must 'snatch out of time the passionate transitory'. Time, for D. H. Lawrence, chosen by Paul Muldoon, is a long telescope.

One of the poets suggested that 'Answering' was a better title for the anthology; but I feel that *Answering Back* has more of the glint, the edge, that some of the new poems here display – U. A. Fanthorpe's response to Walt Whitman being one; Carol Rumens' to Larkin another. Other poems do, less combatively, respond to the initial call, uttering a gentler answering – Liz Lochhead to John Donne – the splash of a stone dropped in a deep well. Some of the new poems are confidently oblique. Some, my own response to Kipling's 'If', the Nation's Favourite Poem, are tongue-in-cheek. *Answering Back* as a title seems to contain the wide range of responses here.

So who is answered and about what? W. H. Auden, Elizabeth Bishop, William Carlos Williams and D. H. Lawrence each have more than one reply in their in-tray. Philip Larkin is twice rebuked. The poet chosen most is John Donne and his great themes of love, belief and death are prominent subjects in the exchanges within this anthology. As Christina Rossetti wrote, 'there is nothing new under the sun.' Or, in the case of several of the poems here, under the moon. What amazed me, once I sat down to choose some kind of order for the hundred poems submitted, was the sense of coherence and community between the living and the dead poets. This sense was so strong, that the dead poets, even the long dead, seemed just as vividly present on the page as the living. I had the feeling I could as easily email Ben Jonson over a typo as I could Craig Raine, who selected him. It was electrifying, as editor, to see how the poems engaged with each other – not only the paired poems, selected and answering, from past and present, but poems who had, as it were, never been formally introduced. There is quite a bit of exchanging of glances across the crowded centuries. I have tried to bring out these connections in the ordering and so, although it is possible to dip in and out of this anthology, the richer experience will be gained by reading it from start to finish.

Poetry, the poets here teach us, is language as life; not only a baton-like passing-on of tradition but a way of making the human immortal. With all their joys, jokes, passions, protests, loves and losses, the poems here prove that it is not only silence that poetry answers back.

CAROL ANN DUFFY

Answering Back

WALTER DE LA MARE

Echo

'Who called?' I said, and the words
    Through the whispering glades,
Hither, thither, baffled the birds –
    'Who called? Who called?'

The leafy boughs on high
    Hissed in the sun;
The dark air carried my cry
    Faintingly on:

Eyes in the green, in the shade,
    In the motionless brake,
Voices that said what I said,
    For mockery's sake:

'Who cares?' I bawled through my tears;
    The wind fell low:
In the silence, 'Who cares? Who cares?'
    Wailed to and fro.

CHOSEN BY *Dannie Abse*

Bluebells

Cycling for the bluebells near St Mellons
two boys tasted the decomposing of the light
in a high echoing tunnel. They stopped,
left foot on the pedal, right on the ground,
to lark loudly, My hen Glad is sad aye!

When Keith shouted I DON'T BELIEVE IN GOD
believe in God . . . in God . . . in God a sudden
WHOOSH replied. Four pupils dilated.
Tachycardia. A goods train clumped over
and multitudinous thunderbolts shrivelled.

Later, bikes angled against a stout tree,
they heard a meandering bee shopping
among the profusion of flowers they bent
to pick. Keith said, Devout little bugger.
Sounds like a daft insect's prayer to me.

Through the returning dark tunnel they hurled
echoes and laughed. But the small dot remained
below the big question mark when they came out
(bluebells alive in the handlebar baskets)
blessed in the unanswering light of the world.

EDWARD THOMAS

Tall Nettles

Tall nettles cover up, as they have done
These many springs, the rusty harrow, the plough
Long worn out, and the roller made of stone:
Only the elm butt tops the nettles now.

This corner of the farmyard I like most:
As well as any bloom upon a flower
I like the dust on the nettles, never lost
Except to prove the sweetness of a shower.

CHOSEN BY *Gillian Clarke*

4

GILLIAN CLARKE

Nettles

for Edward Thomas

No old machinery, no tangled chains
of a harrow locked in rust and rising grasses,
nor the fallen stones of ancient habitation
where nettles feed on what we leave behind.
Nothing but an old compost heap
warmed to a simmer of sickly pungency,
lawn clippings we never moved, but meant to,

and can't, now, because nettles have moved in,
and it's a poet's words inhabit this.
And, closer, look! The stems lean with the weight,
the young of peacock butterflies, just hatched,
their glittering black spines and spots of pearl.
And I want to say to the dead, look what a poet sings
to life: the bite of nettles, caterpillars, wings.

WILLIAM CARLOS WILLIAMS

The Red Wheelbarrow

so much depends
upon

a red wheel
barrow

glazed with rain
water

beside the white
chickens

CHOSEN BY *Ian McMillan*

The Green Wheelbarrow

To be honest, not much depends on this.
My dad just left it by the side of the lawn
When he went to pick me up after I fell.

His spade and fork sat in it waiting
For him to return; like my mother
Sat looking through the window

Each night, waiting for him to come home
From the office, like she'd waited for him
To come back from the sea.

Winter nights, the rain glazed the road,
It turned to snow, flakes floating
Like the feathers of chickens.

My dad picked me up and I stopped crying.
I'm crying now, dad. I wish
I could sit by the window and see you coming home.

Go on, push the wheelbarrow again!
Let me hear the music of the squeak!

PHILIP LARKIN

This Be The Verse

They fuck you up, your mum and dad.
They may not mean to, but they do.
They fill you with the faults they had
And add some extra, just for you.

But they were fucked up in their turn
By fools in old-style hats and coats,
Who half the time were soppy stern
And half at one another's throats,

Man hands on misery to man.
It deepens like a coastal shelf.
Get out as early as you can,
And don't have any kids yourself.

CHOSEN BY *Carol Rumens*

CAROL RUMENS

This Be The Verse

(Philip Larkin)

Not everybody's
    Childhood sucked:
There are some kiddies
    Not up-fucked.

They moan and shout,
    Won't take advice.
But – hang about –
    Most turn out nice –

If not better
    Than us, no worse.
Sad non-begetter,
    That bean't the verse.

DYLAN THOMAS

In My Craft or Sullen Art

In my craft or sullen art
Exercised in the still night
When only the moon rages
And the lovers lie abed
With all their griefs in their arms,
I labour by singing light
Not for ambition or bread
Or the strut and trade of charms
On the ivory stages
But for the common wages
Of their most secret heart.

Not for the proud man apart
From the raging moon I write
On these spindrift pages
Nor for the towering dead
With their nightingales and psalms
But for the lovers, their arms
Round the griefs of the ages,
Who pay no heed or wages
Nor heed my craft or art.

CHOSEN BY *Nina Cassian*

My Last Book

How do I know
that this is my last book?
My genes are adamant.
My energy longs for exhaustion.
The words tell me to shut up.
Yet, in total silence,
my crippled hand
ejects sometimes a pen
to inject a poem
like a shot, an intravenous,
in the missing arm of Venus.

TOMAS TRANSTRÖMER

translated from Swedish by Robert Bly

Allegro

After a black day, I play Haydn,
and feel a little warmth in my hands.

The keys are ready. Kind hammers fall.
The sound is spirited, green, and full of silence.

The sound says that freedom exists
and someone pays no taxes to Caesar.

I shove my hands in my haydnpockets
and act like a man who is calm about it all.

I raise my haydnflag. The signal is:
'We do not surrender. But want peace.'

The music is a house of glass standing on a slope;
rocks are flying, rocks are rolling.

The rocks roll straight through the house
but every pane of glass is still whole.

CHOSEN BY *Robin Robertson*

ROBIN ROBERTSON

Ictus

for Tomas Tranströmer

I find myself at your side, turning
the pages for you – haltingly – with my
wrong hand, while you play
those delicate, certain notes
without effort, sounding a long
free line through the sea-lanes on the skiff
of your moving hand: your only hand,
your whole right side snowbound.

Who would swap the hammer
for the hammer-blow, the seasons
for this wintering life, that
lethal fold in time? No one I know.
But you have made an art
of setting a logan-stone rocking
here in Södermalm, and learnt the perfect
stress of lines, and ferry-times, by heart.

I find I can suddenly read the score, know
when to turn the page: *citeog*,
cack-handed, my dull heart-tick always
indicating left. Sunlight squares the room
and I am snowblind. You slip away
on the wind. Your grandfather,
the pilot, stares out over the archipelago
from his solid wooden frame.

ictus: metrical stress/the beat of the pulse/a stroke, seizure
citeog (Gaelic; pronounced *kitog*): left-handed
cack-handed: clumsy/left-handed.

The Clock

Bright and early, fine intent,
I sing, since life is easy,
To the fine town by Rhiw Rheon
Near the rock, with the round fort.
There, she was once renowned,
Is one who used to know me.
Salutations here today
To the worthy woman's dwelling:
Nightly, discreet noble girl,
That maiden seems to greet me.

One bent on sleep, exhausted,
It's a dream, needless to say,
My head upon a pillow,
Yonder comes, before the day,
Into plain sight an image,
A dear angel in a girl's bed.
I'd thought, my mind deep in sleep,
I was then with my sweetheart:
Far from me, memory seeks her,
Was her face when I woke up.

Woe's the clock beside the dyke,
Black its face, that awoke me.
May its head and tongue be worthless
And its two ropes and its wheel,
And its weights, idiotic balls,
And its framework and its hammer,
And its ducks thinking it's daytime,
And its never-resting mills.
Rude clock like a drunken cobbler's

Foolish clacking, cursed be its time,
Deceitful untruthful entrails,
Puppy dog gnawing a bowl,
Frequent clapper in monks' cloister,
Goblin mill grinding by night.
Has saddler with scabby rump
Or tiler been more unsteady?
A deadly curse on its cry
For snatching me here from heaven

I was having, comforting sign,
A heavenly sleep at midnight,
In her slender arms enfolded,
Held between a Deifr's breasts.
Will there be seen, grief's nurture,
Land's Eigr, such a sight again?

Run straightway to her once more,
Dream, yours no luckless journey:
Ask the girl beneath gold thatching
Will she herself come tonight
To give, heart of gold, a vision
Sun's niece, just for once, of her?

CHOSEN BY *Menna Elfyn*

MENNA ELFYN *translated from Welsh by Gillian Clarke*

A Dream Against the Clock

Midsummer night
And his words woke me
Like the car-struck cat.
He sang alive in my ear
And I, nimble with wakefulness.

Came the dreamer himself
Walking, an old clock's feet,
Pendulum rocking to and fro,
Ebb and flow, letting go,
My limbs creating a world,
My face lovely with dreaming,
Facing my fantasy,
Facing the question:
When does beauty die?

Our clock is our havoc.
A moment's glance, and desire's
What we see from the bed.

Then I walked asleep,
My body burning, restless,
Every door in the night-grove
Was a heavy foot treading.
In summer woods I wandered with Dafydd:
He gave me aloes and almonds,
A May full of cinnamon,
Leaves of a thousand vanillas,
Five rustlings of the body's harvest.

Till Time's voice brought me back
From the green grove.
The tell-tale clock shamed me,
Caught me out pleasuring,
Ticking, tocking, leaving
The lover's house of leaves.

The old story, I know. In my winter-house
I'll make my own nest at summer's end.
Come the time, as it comes to us all,
To seek the enchantment of sleep,
For the breath playing its lute.
My dream under the eaves
Came to me, but broke its promise.

WALLACE STEVENS

Fabliau of Florida

Barque of phosphor
On the palmy beach,

Move outward into heaven,
Into the alabasters
And night blues.

Foam and cloud are one.
Sultry moon-monsters
Are dissolving.

Fill your black hull
With white moonlight.

There will never be an end
To this droning of the surf.

<small>CHOSEN BY</small> *Sean O'Brien*

Grey Bayou

When I return to Grey Bayou, the mud-kingdom
Fed by dykes and chalky run-off
I would like my fire-ship to nose ashore

Beside the sheds near Little Switzerland
In memory of lust among the quarry-pits
A thousand years ago, before the bridge.

It is roads now, clover-leafs, pillars,
And only the bayou remains of that world,
Its reed-beds caged against the shifting channels,

Though the eternal flame to industry still burns,
Tiny like a welder's torch, far off
Downriver on the southern side, among the palms.

I would like a flotilla of tar-coloured barges
To happen past then, inbound for Goole,
The odd crewman furtively smoking and staring,

As though an ancient prophecy is vindicated
Just when the fools who denied it are dead or in jail:
For this is the place, the rivermen know,

In which nothing need happen especially.
A boat burning out on the flats
Belongs with one more fording on horseback,

The first cries of love in the elder-grove,
Dark mild and cigarettes, the Mississippian
Expanses of the unknown Grey Bayou,

Its grey-brown tides, its skies
That dwarf the bridge and with their vast
Indifference properly invoke the gods.

D. H. LAWRENCE

Humming-Bird

I can imagine, in some otherworld
Primeval-dumb, far back
In that most awful stillness, that only gasped and hummed,
Humming-birds raced down the avenues.

Before anything had a soul,
While life was a heave of Matter, half inanimate,
This little bit chipped off in brilliance
And went whizzing through the slow, vast succulent stems.

I believe there were no flowers then,
In the world where humming-bird flashed ahead of creation.
I believe he pierced the slow vegetable veins with his long beak.

Probably he was big
As mosses, and little lizards, they say, were once big.
Probably he was a jabbing, terrifying monster.

We look at him through the wrong end of the long telescope of Time,
Luckily for us.

CHOSEN BY *Paul Muldoon*

A Hummingbird

At Nora's first post-divorce Labor Day bash
there's a fluster and a fuss and a fidget
in the fuchsia-bells. 'Two fingers of sour mash,
a maraschino cherry.' 'So the digit's
still a unit of measurement?' 'While midgets
continue to demand a slice of the cake.'
'A vibrator, you know, *that* kind of widget.'
Now a ruby-throated hummingbird remakes
itself as it rolls on through mid-forest brake.
'I'm guessing she's had a neck-lift *and* lipo.'
'You know I still can't help but think of the *Wake*
as the apogee, you know, of the typo.'
Like an engine rolling on after a crash,
long after whatever it was made a splash.

Travel

The railroad track is miles away,
And the day is loud with voices speaking.
Yet there isn't a train goes by all day
But I hear its whistle shrieking.

All night there isn't a train goes by,
Though the night is still for sleep and dreaming,
But I see its cinders red on the sky,
And hear its engine steaming.

My heart is warm with the friends I make,
And better friends I'll not be knowing;
Yet there isn't a train I wouldn't take,
No matter where it's going.

CHOSEN BY *Roger McGough*

ROGER McGOUGH

Quiet Zone

(Poem for a lady on the Bristol to Paddington train, who spent the journey in the 'Quiet Coach', chatting on her mobile phone.)

With respect, this is the quiet zone.
And although when travelling on your own
it's nice to have a good old chat
with someone on the phone
this is the quiet zone.

'*Shhhh* . . . *Quiet!*' say the signs
on every table, window and door
obviously nothing to do with mobiles
so what do you think they're for?

A warning perhaps to brass bands
looking for a place to rehearse?
To the horde of angry soccer fans
who need to stamp and curse?
A troop of soldiers on the march
tramp, tramp. Or worse?
A stampede of trumpeting elephants?
A disruptive class of kids?
The entire cast of *Stomp* banging dustbin lids?
A volcano bursting to erupt?
An unexploded mine?

'*Shhhh* . . . *Quiet!*' With respect,
can't you read the sign?

ALLEN GINSBERG

from Howl

(for Carl Solomon)

I saw the best minds of my generation destroyed by madness,
    starving hysterical naked,
dragging themselves through the negro streets at dawn looking for
    an angry fix,
angelheaded hipsters burning for the ancient heavenly connection
    to the starry dynamo in the machinery of night,
who poverty and tatters and hollow-eyed and high sat up smoking
    in the supernatural darkness of cold-water flats floating across
    the tops of cities contemplating jazz,
who bared their brains to Heaven under the El and saw
    Mohammedan angels staggering on tenement roofs illuminated,
who passed through universities with radiant cool eyes
    hallucinating Arkansas and Blake-light tragedy among the
    scholars of war,
who were expelled from the academies for crazy & publishing
    obscene odes on the windows of the skull,
who cowered in unshaven rooms in underwear, burning their
    money in wastebaskets and listening to the Terror through the
    wall.

CHOSEN BY *Tony Curtis*

TONY CURTIS

Trowel

After Allen Ginsberg

I have seen the best minds of my generation destroyed by DIY.

WALT WHITMAN

The Beasts

I think I could turn and live with animals, they are so placid and
    self-contain'd;
I stand and look at them long and long.
They do not sweat and whine about their condition;
They do not lie awake in the dark and weep for their sins;
They do not make me sick discussing their duty to God;
Not one is dissatisfied – not one is demented with the mania of
    owning things;
Not one kneels to another, nor to his kind that lived thousands
    of years ago;
Not one is respectable or industrious over the whole earth.

CHOSEN BY *U. A. Fanthorpe*

A Word, Camerade . . .

I know I couldn't bear it, to live with the animals.
You look 'long and long' – but you've clearly not seen
A horse's eye's consternation, or the shivering
Noses of deer. And as for that stuff about God and sin –
Any careful cow would know you're not thinking of her,
Just pleased with your atheist self. You've only to open your eyes
To discern a disconsolate pig. Owning things? Mania? Dementia
    (What words
You know!) Distress of a sheep whose lamb's lost –
Have you never noticed that? When you're
Soppily brooding on animals you're just having
A cheap little go at God.
                        You reckless old drop-out, you
Inventor of abattoirs, factory farms – it's people like you
Who make beasts afraid. Just look a bit harder. Try *thinking*.

W. H. AUDEN

Musée des Beaux Arts

About suffering they were never wrong,
The Old Masters: how well they understood
Its human position; how it takes place
While someone else is eating or opening a window or just walking
    dully along;
How, when the aged are reverently, passionately waiting
For the miraculous birth, there always must be
Children who did not specially want it to happen, skating
On a pond at the edge of the wood:

They never forgot
That even the dreadful martyrdom must run its course
Anyhow in a corner, some untidy spot
Where the dogs go on with their doggy life and the torturer's horse
Scratches its innocent behind on a tree.

In Brueghel's *Icarus*, for instance: how everything turns away
Quite leisurely from the disaster; the ploughman may
Have heard the splash, the forsaken cry,
But for him it was not an important failure; the sun shone
As it had to on the white legs disappearing into the green
Water; and the expensive delicate ship that must have seen
Something amazing, a boy falling out of the sky,
Had somewhere to get to and sailed calmly on.

CHOSEN BY *Billy Collins*

BILLY COLLINS

Musée des Beaux Arts Revisited

As far as mental anguish goes,
the old painters were no fools.
They understood how the mind,
the freakiest dungeon in the castle,
can effortlessly imagine a crab with the face of a priest
or an end table complete with genitals.

And they knew that the truly monstrous
lies not so much in the wildly shocking,
a skeleton spinning a wheel of fire, say,
but in the small prosaic touch
added to a tableau of the hellish,
the detail at the heart of the horrid.

In Bosch's *The Temptation of St. Anthony*
for instance, how it is not so much
the boar-faced man in the pea-green dress
that frightens, but the white mandolin he carries,
not the hooded corpse in a basket
but the way the basket is rigged to hang from a bare branch;

how, what must have driven St. Anthony
to the mossy brink of despair
was not the big, angry-looking fish
in the central panel,
the one with the two mouse-like creatures
conferring on its tail,
but rather what the fish is wearing:

a kind of pale orange officer's cape
and, over that,
a metal body-helmet secured by silvery wires,
a sensible buckled chin strap,
and, yes, the ultimate test of faith –
the tiny sword that hangs from the thing,
that nightmare carp,
secure in its brown leather scabbard.

LOUIS MACNEICE

The Suicide

And this, ladies and gentlemen, whom I am not in fact
Conducting, was his office all those minutes ago,
This man you never heard of. There are the bills
In his intray, the ash in the ashtray, the grey memoranda stacked
Against him, the serried ranks of the box-files, the packed
Jury of his unanswered correspondence
Nodding under the paperweight in the breeze
From the window by which he left; and here is the cracked
Receiver that never got mended and here is the jotter
With his last doodle which might be his own digestive tract
Ulcer and all or might be the flowery maze
Through which he had wandered deliciously till he stumbled
Suddenly finally conscious of all he lacked
On a manhole under the hollyhocks. The pencil
Point had obviously broken, yet, when he left this room
By catdrop sleight-of-foot or simple vanishing act,
To those who knew him for all that mess in the street
This man with the shy smile has left behind
Something that was intact.

CHOSEN BY *Colette Bryce*

The Manager

The office after dark shifts
in a streetlamp atmospheric,
a cornery mind
turned in on itself,
seeming to find
a quietness.

Blinds hang at half mast.
Closed door. Shut drawers.
Strip-bulbs slumber
in their casings.
The radiator cools in pangs.

Seen from out there in the night,
it is a note extinguished
in the skyline.

Inside is an amber spell,
a window's Rothko repeat
on the opposite wall.

Hard footsteps fade
in the echoey corridor.

An anglepoise in silhouette
suspends above the desk
in a short-sighted scrutiny,
a hermit's hood or bell.

That cabinet, the heart, boom
boom, with its hoard
of duplicates.

The terminal, a squat god,
is expressionless,
its pinpoint pulse
evidence
of something else.

The chair twirls on its stalk, its foot
an asterisk on plastic castors;
what is he doing
sitting there in the dark
in any case?
Perhaps he's lost it.

The bucket of black is only a bin,
a bluish gleam around the rim.

The scribble of leads at his feet,
though it seems to writhe, is not
a pit of snakes.

Get up. Go home.
It is time for the setting
of alarms, for codes and keypads,
hairspring triggers.

A sudden sweep illumination:
the swift cloth of headlights
wiping the walls,
then gone.

From the street, the clatter
of shutters going down.

THOMAS HARDY

She Saw Him, She Said

'Why, I saw you with the sexton, outside the church-door,
    So I did not hurry me home,
    Thinking you'd not be come,
    Having something to him to say. –
Yes: 'twas you, Dear, though you seemed sad, heart-sore;
    How fast you've got therefrom!'

'I've not been out. I've watched the moon through the birch,
    And heard the bell toll. Yes,
    Like a passing soul in distress!'
    ' – But no bell's tolled to-day?' . . .
His face looked strange, like the face of him seen by the church,
    And she sank to musefulness.

CHOSEN BY *Roy Fisher*

ROY FISHER

A Mellstock Fiddle

By the road where seldom aught would pass
Save a hearse
He'd, gazing through the blear of the glass,
His comfort seek in verse.

Strange, though, when at the thought of rhyme
Troubles he'd store for himself
As his notebook at an accustomed time
He'd pluck from its trim shelf.

'Twas as though within that withering heart
Some tuneless din
Told what might rule once done was art.
A cat. A biscuit-tin.

JOHN DONNE

From: **Holy Sonnets**

Death be not proud, though some have called thee
Mighty and dreadfull, for, thou art not soe,
For, those, whom thou think'st, thou dost overthrow,
Die not, poore death, nor yet canst thou kill mee;
From rest and sleepe, which but thy pictures bee,
Much pleasure, then from thee, much more must flow,
And soonest our best men with thee doe goe,
Rest of their bones, and soules deliverie.
Thou art slave to Fate, chance, kings, and desperate men,
And dost with poyson, warre, and sicknesse dwell,
And poppie, or charmes can make us sleepe as well,
And better than thy stroake; why swell'st thou then?
One short sleepe past, wee wake eternally,
And death shall be no more; death, thou shalt die.

CHOSEN BY *Vernon Scannell*

Another View of Thanatos

Death be not proud! Why not? You've got good cause.
Mighty and dreadful? Yes, we're bound to call
You both of these since you have fathered all
Our best achievements, art and healing, laws,
Rituals to ease the pain that gnaws
On hearts and minds till desperations scrawl
Their shrill graffiti on the falling wall:
You justly claim respect, if not applause.

But few of us will tender thanks though you
Persuade us to erect great domes of thought
And palisades of piety to thwart
Your fruitful menaces. Yet this is true:
You frighten me to death, old sport;
If I had half your power, then I'd swank too.

A. E. HOUSMAN

From: A Shropshire Lad

Loveliest of trees, the cherry now
Is hung with bloom along the bough,
And stands about the woodland ride
Wearing white for Eastertide.

Now, of my threescore years and ten,
Twenty will not come again,
And take from seventy springs a score,
It only leaves me fifty more.

And since to look at things in bloom
Fifty springs are little room,
About the woodlands I will go
To see the cherry hung with snow.

CHOSEN BY *Wendy Cope*

Reading Housman

Reading Housman, knowing he
Ran out of springs and will not see
Another flowering cherry tree,
I sniff and wipe away a tear.
Then Molesworth mutters in my ear,
Does peotry make you blub, my dere?

W. B. YEATS

The Lake Isle of Innisfree

I will arise and go now, and go to Innisfree,
And a small cabin build there, of clay and wattles made;
Nine bean rows will I have there, a hive for the honey bee,
    And live alone in the bee-loud glade.

And I shall have some peace there, for peace comes dropping slow,
Dropping from the veils of the morning to where the cricket sings;
There midnight's all a-glimmer, and noon a purple glow,
    And evening full of the linnet's wings.

I will arise and go now, for always night and day
I hear lake water lapping with low sounds by the shore;
While I stand on the roadway, or on the pavement grey,
    I hear it in the deep heart's core.

CHOSEN BY *R. V. Bailey*

R. V. BAILEY

On Leaving the Lake Isle of Innisfree

I'm leaving the Isle of Innisfree.
I never liked it much:
The little clay and wattle hutch
Was far too small for me.

The bees? They stung me, left and right.
The beans got black-fly (and other things).
The noise of the crickets and linnets' wings
Kept me awake all night.

I've had it with water lapping on shore;
I'm homesick for proper plumbing.
I'm randy for tarmac and taxis galore,

. . . And I've a *Guardian* poem coming.

C. P. CAVAFY

translated from Greek by Edmund Keeley and Philip Sherrard

Ithaka

As you set out for Ithaka
hope your road is a long one,
full of adventure, full of discovery.
Laistrygonians, Cyclops,
angry Poseidon – don't be afraid of them:
you'll never find things like that on your way
as long as you keep your thoughts raised high,
as long as a rare excitement
stirs your spirit and your body.
Laistrygonians, Cyclops,
wild Poseidon – you won't encounter them
unless you bring them along inside your soul,
unless your soul sets them up in front of you.

Hope your road is a long one.
May there be many summer mornings when,
with what pleasure, what joy,
you enter harbours you're seeing for the first time;
may you stop at Phoenician trading stations
to buy fine things,
mother of pearl and coral, amber and ebony,
sensual perfume of every kind –
as many sensual perfumes as you can;
and may you visit many Egyptian cities
to learn and go on learning from their scholars.

Keep Ithaka always in your mind.
Arriving there is what you're destined for.
But don't hurry the journey at all.
Better if it lasts for years,
so you're old by the time you reach the island,
wealthy with all you've gained on the way,
not expecting Ithaka to make you rich.

Ithaka gave you the marvellous journey.
Without her you wouldn't have set out.
She has nothing left to give you now.
And if you find her poor, Ithaka won't have fooled you.
Wise as you will have become, so full of experience,
you'll have understood by then what these Ithakas mean.

CHOSEN BY *Theo Dorgan*

Ithacafor

for Leonard Cohen

When you set out from Ithaca again,
let it be autumn, early, the plane leaves falling as you go,
for spring would shake you with its quickening,
its whispers of youth.

You will have earned the road down to the harbour,
duty discharged, your toll of labour paid,
the house four-square, your son in the full of fatherhood,
his mother, your long-beloved, gone to the shades.

Walk by the doorways, do not look left or right,
do not inhale the woodsmoke,
the shy glow of the young girls,
the resin and pine of home.
Allow them permit you to leave,
they have been good neighbours.

Plank fitted to plank, slow work and sure,
the mast straight as your back.
Water and wine, oil, salt and bread.
Take a hand in yours for luck.

Cast off the lines without a backward glance
and sheet in the sail.
There will be harbours, shelter from weather,
there will be long empty passages far from land.
There may be love or kindness, do not count on this
but allow for possibility.
Be ready for storms.

When you take leave of Ithaca, round to the south
then strike far down for Circe, Calypso,
what you remember, what you must keep in mind.
Trust to your course, long since laid down for you.
There was never any question of turning back.
All those who came the journey with you,
those who fell to the flash of bronze,
those who turned away into other fates,
are long gathered to asphodel and dust.
You will go uncompanioned, but go you must.

There will be time in the long days and nights,
stunned by the sun or driven by the stars,
to unwind your spool of life.
You will learn again what you always knew –
the wind sweeps everything away.

When you set out from Ithaca again
you will not need to ask where you are going.
Give every day your full, unselfconscious attention –
the rise and flash of the swell on your beam,
the lift into small harbours –
and do not forget Ithaca, keep Ithaca in your mind.
All that it was and is, and will be without you.

Be grateful for where you have been,
for those who kept to your side,
those who strode out ahead of you
or stood back and watched you sail away.
Be grateful for kindness in the perfumed dark
but sooner or later you will sail out again.

Some morning, some clear night
you will come to the Pillars of Hercules.
Sail through if you wish. You are free to turn back.
Go forward on deck, lay your hand on the mast,
hear the wind in its dipping branches.
Now you are free of home and journeying,
rocked on the cusp of tides.
Ithaca is before you, Ithaca is behind you.
Man is born homeless, and shaped for the sea.
You must do what is best.

WILLIAM CARLOS WILLIAMS

Labrador

How clean these shadows
how firm these rocks stand
about which wash
the waters of the world.

It is ice to this body
that unclothes its pallors
to thoughts
of an immeasurable sea,

unmarred, that as it lifts
enclosing this
straining mind, these
limbs in a single gesture.

CHOSEN BY *Ruth Padel*

Svalbard

Suddenly a bang. Field-gun crack of a ten-thousand-year-old
bubble released. Water has eaten the island's underhang.
Boring in glacier archives we find carbony bindweed
underneath high Arctic ice. Thin line

of Brannich's guillemots zips up the gold horizon.
Ice was always the boss. What do we do with the mind
that patted itself on the back, knew it was a bit of a bastard
but richer for the devil in it; always redeemed via *religio*,

meaning 'a tie'? And Nature, unmeasured
Creation, was mirror: the made-for-me Eden
dizzy with my presence, washed clean
by the waters of world. Look – milk-gothic spires

slip away to translucence and such zooplankton
as still bloom for krill in this sea, sending gold waves
to a shore where tidewater glaciers unleaven like loaves
deliquescing back into dough. A snow flake falls.

Smack of water displaced. Putting one green blue
step after the other, what can you do with a cracked
reflection, pushing heels into snow to keep upright,
keep balance, cling to the very idea of protection?

Unfold Your Own Myth

Who gets up early to discover the moment light begins?
Who finds us here circling, bewildered, like atoms?
Who comes to a spring thirsty
and sees the moon reflected in it?
Who, like Jacob blind with grief and age,
smells the shirt of his lost son
and can see again?
Who lets a bucket down and brings up
a flowing prophet? Or like Moses goes for fire
and finds what burns inside the sunrise?

Jesus slips into a house to escape enemies
and opens a door to the other world.
Solomon cuts open a fish, and there's a gold ring.
Omar storms in to kill the prophet
and leaves with blessings.
Chase a deer and end up everywhere!
An oyster opens his mouth to swallow one drop.
Now there's a pearl.
A vagrant wanders empty ruins.
Suddenly he's wealthy.

But don't be satisfied with stories, how things
have gone with others. Unfold
your own myth, without complicated explanations,
so everyone will understand the passage,
We have opened you.

Start walking towards Shams. Your legs will get heavy
and tired. Then comes a moment
of feeling the wings you've grown,
lifting.

CHOSEN BY *Imtiaz Dharker*

Myth

The books promised paradise. A taxi-driver
pointed out the way, past
the traffic-lights, beyond the billboards,
second right. We hoped
we might soon see the tops of trees
haloed in ethereal light.

Not this. Not this.
The everyday. These giant screens
hoisted at street-corners, making
noisy promises. These flags
drifting through the avenues, looking
for a place to settle. Thin
plastic bags puffed up with empty air.

No paradise, this, where lost
souls cry in mobile phones.
A curtain shifts. I freeze.
I have strayed into unknown myths,
every shape a threat.
I shield my eyes, hold up the mirror
to reveal the shrouded enemy. The frost
of my own breath mists the glass

and clears to show
no demon, no terror, no forked tongue,
no head of hissing snakes,
no can of worms, but

only the face I know,
my neighbour, my sister.

The grace of the familiar,
The blessed.
The everyday.

*

The mist of my breath
slides off the angled mirror
to reveal your face.

*

All night, my face next
to your mouth, I hold my breath,
listening to yours.

*

A circus of stars,
your dreams a trapeze, faces
lift like mirrored moons.

*

Hung above your sleep,
Low moon on your horizon,
My heart grows immense.

Insomnia

The moon in the bureau mirror
looks out a million miles
(and perhaps with pride, at herself,
but she never, never smiles)
far and away beyond sleep, or
perhaps she's a daytime sleeper.

By the Universe deserted
she'd tell it to go to hell,
and she'd find a body of water,
or a mirror, on which to dwell.
So wrap up care in a cobweb
and drop it down the well

into that world inverted
where left is always right,
where the shadows are really the body,
where we stay awake all night,
where the heavens are shallow as the sea
is now deep, and you love me.

CHOSEN BY *Ruth Fainlight*

Insomniac's Moon

Insomniac's moon,
mineral and organic,
with its phosphorescent
mushroom-punky glow,
its halo of acid orange
rim of gassy blue

the blue and orange
that flash from a prism
or the bevelled facets
stabbing that image
into sleepless eyes
from a mirror's edge,

like a drop of milk
pearling from the breast
of the harsh moon-mother
which I try to catch
between parted lips
before it dissolves

with other ancient dreams
of love and sleep,
or the blue and orange
of fading bruises,
into the oceanic dark
circling the universe.

W. S. GILBERT

The Captain's Song (*H.M.S. Pinafore*)

Fair moon, to thee I sing,
   Bright regent of the heavens,
Say, why is everything
   Either at sixes or at sevens?
I have lived hitherto
   Free from breath of slander
Beloved by all my crew
   A really popular commander,
But now my kindly crew rebel,
   My daughter to a tar is partial.
Sir Joseph storms and, sad to tell,
   He threatens a court martial!
Fair moon, to thee I sing,
   Bright regent of the heavens,
Say, why is everything
   Either at sixes or at sevens?

BUTTERCUP: How sweetly he carols forth his melody to the
unconscious moon!

CHOSEN BY *Jenny Joseph*

JENNY JOSEPH

The Worshipful Company of Moonwatchers

Among moon gazers there may be one
Who has disappeared from among us under years of sense and
    sanity,
Joined those who sleep behind curtains, drawn so thick
No light will wake him until the hour he appointed.
His evenings are spent on what he planned to do;
His early mornings are preparation for the day.

And then, after an illness perhaps, he is back,
As surprised as we are each time, when, after an absence –
An interval wrapped away in our other lives –
We are surprised by the moon. He is back
Moon-watching again; gets up in the night, to the window
And sees the effects of a great wind pouring
Rushing like a tide sweeping through the belt of trees.
It tosses the ship of cloud that bears the effulgence
Lighting up the busyness of this high world,
The life his sleeping household, dreaming children
And the street and whole town of safe, shut little houses
Are oblivious to.

Now once again he is out under the moon,
After the ghostly galleons of all our childhoods
The betrayed lovers' moon we have crooned and sighed to
The hunter's, bomber's moon enabling death
The harvest moon that made night day for the farmers
And ended entangled in a hawthorn hedge
Like a huge football we could run to and touch.
He has gone down into the strange night garden
To watch her travel, her woe-begone face
Shifting behind the contrary wisps of cloud;
And it is as though all these moons are there:
The moon becalmed among flocked clouds,
Then suddenly reigning alone in an empty deep sky.
The moon glittering on the sea, lands away,
The little moon as frail as arrowed plane tracks
Dissolving in a summer dawn.
The blue cold wash off sterile mountains, the malign overseer
Of night fevers, peers into his dreams;
Something is there
Behind his shoulder, outside the window, at the back of the door.
He knows he has been pulled into the moon's orbit, then into her
     circle,
That he is in that air other than
The air of day.
The realm of faery, it was one time called

Where fantasy is bred, and desire shakes through the body
And the moon draws her net, pulling the tides
Of the land as she does of the sea.

JOHN DONNE

A Nocturnall Upon S. Lucies Day

BEING THE SHORTEST DAY*

Tis the yeares midnight, and it is the dayes,
Lucies, who scarce seaven houres herself unmaskes,
   The Sunne is spent, and now his flasks
   Send forth light squibs, no constant rayes;
      The worlds whole sap is sunke:
The generall balme th'hydroptique earth hath drunk,
Whither, as to the beds-feet, life is shrunke,
Dead and enterr'd; yet all these seeme to laugh,
Compar'd with mee, who am their Epitaph.

Study me then, you who shall lovers bee
At the next world, that is, at the next Spring:
   For I am every dead thing,
   In whom love wrought new Alchimie.
      For his art did expresse
A quintessence even from nothingnesse,
From dull privations, and leane emptinesse
He ruin'd mee, and I am re-begot
Of absence, darknesse, death; things which are not.

All others, from all things, draw all that's good,
Life, soule, forme, spirit, whence they beeing have;
   I, by loves limbecke, am the grave
   Of all, that's nothing. Oft a flood
      Have wee two wept, and so

* 13 December (12 December O.S., according to the old calendar.
22 December N.S.), the day of the Winter Solstice, when the sun
enters the sign of Capricorn (*v.* l. 39).

Drownd the whole world, us two; oft did we grow
To be two Chaosses, when we did show
Care to ought else; and often absences
Withdrew our soules, and made us carcasses.

But I am by her death, (which word wrongs her)
Of the first nothing, the Elixer grown;
    Were I a man, that I were one,
    I needs must know; I should preferre,
        If I were any beast,
Some ends, some means; Yea plants, yea stones detest,
And love; All, all some properties invest;
If I an ordinary nothing were,
As shadow, a light, and body must be here.

But I am None; nor will my Sunne renew.
You lovers, for whose sake, the lesser Sunne
    At this time to the Goat is runne
    To fetch new lust, and give it you,
        Enjoy your summer all;
Since shee enjoyes her long nights festivall,
Let mee prepare towards her, and let mee call
This houre her Vigill, and her Eve, since this
Both the yeares, and the dayes deep midnight is.

CHOSEN BY *Liz Lochhead*

62

Midwinter Song

At midday on the year's midnight
into my mind came
I saw the new moon late yestreen
wi the auld moon in her airms though no
there is no moon of course,
there's nothing very much of anything to speak of
in the sky except a gey dreich greyness
rain-laden over Glasgow and today
there is the very least of even this for us to get
but
the light comes back
the light always comes back
and this begins tomorrow with however many minutes
more of sun and serotonin.
Meanwhile
there will be the winter moon for us to love the longest,
fat in the frosty sky among the sharpest stars,
and lines of old songs we can't remember why we know
or when first we heard them will aye come back
once in a blue moon to us
unbidden, bless us with their long-travelled light.

GIACOMO LEOPARDI

translated from Italian by Eamon Grennan

To the Moon

Now that the year has come full circle,
I remember climbing this hill, heartbroken,
To gaze up at the graceful sight of you,
And how you hung then above those woods
As you do tonight, bathing them in brightness.
But at that time your face seemed nothing
But a cloudy shimmering through my tears,
So wretched was the life I led: and lead still . . .
Nothing changes, moon of my delight. Yet
I find pleasure in recollection, in calling back
My season of grief: when one is young,
And hope is a long road, memory
A short one, how welcome then
The remembrance of things past – no matter
How sad, and the heart still grieving

CHOSEN BY *Julie O'Callaghan*

64

JULIE O'CALLAGHAN

Alla Luna

a lunar cycle

Last summer
we lived
on the planet
of purest sadness
looking at people
in the streets
like aliens –
looking at each day
as if it were the last.
We spoke to the moon
without words,
without hope.

*

There was a blue pool
in the sky.
We liked swimming
up there when the moon
and some stars
floated in the water.
You had to be careful
not to butterfly
through a cloud
or dog paddle
into the universe.

*

What was the deal last summer?
We were surrounded
by sky in all directions.
If it wasn't dawn over the lake
it was dusk over the buildings.
Not to mention lightning,
orbiting sky furniture
like stars, planets,
then examining the moon
through your telescope.
All we ever did
was try to sit still
holding our breath
watching the heavens
for a sign.

*

Oh really –
let's all gaze at the moon
and have a nervous breakdown
since life stinks.
I was looking at the lake sideways,
my head on a pillow
wishing and wishing
you would get better.
The moon went blurry:
space-garbage sneering
at me and my sadness.

*

A year ago
I stood at the window
high in the sky crying.
I focused my father's telescope,
saw lunar mountains, craters, valleys.
'Well, moon,' I said,
'how can I ever be happy again
when my father is disappearing
to a place I can't visualise?'
Luna, I watched you change
all summer into a harvest moon
just before he died.

*

If you were still
in this solar system
we'd be e-mailing
comet sightings
to each other like crazy
and you'd have flipped
watching Hale–Bopp
through your skyscraper windows
on Sheridan Road.
But now I guess
you're some kind of asteroid yourself
travelling to wherever.
Great timing, Jack.
You're missing everything.

THOMAS HARDY

The Voice

Woman much missed, how you call to me, call to me,
Saying that now you are not as you were
When you had changed from the one who was all to me,
But as at first, when our day was fair.

Can it be you that I hear? Let me view you, then,
Standing as when I drew near to the town
Where you would wait for me: yes, as I knew you then,
Even to the original air-blue gown!

Or is it only the breeze, in its listnessness
Travelling across the wet mead to me here,
You being ever dissolved to wan wistlessness,
Heard no more again far or near?

    Thus I; faltering forward,
    Leaves around me falling,
Wind oozing thin through the thorn from norward,
    And the woman calling.

CHOSEN BY *Henry Shukman*

The Call

All these years and I still don't understand
how it works, how the signal gets through
the bones of my hand, the bricks of this house,
the bank building opposite, and across

miles of suburb and field, pylons and roads,
hills and four rivers to precisely you,
in another city, another house, another room,
hunched by the bath with your phone in your hand,

sobbing. You can't bear to feel so split,
you gasp. Downstairs you hear
a chair scrape, a man's voice.
He laughs, in dialogue with a ghost.

But I understand how light works.
Earlier your back gleamed like a guitar.
The last leaves on the sycamore
flickered like a school of mackerel.

Later I will go out in a leopard-coat of light
without you: just me and the trees baring themselves
for winter, and the marbled paving stones,
and my empty hand shining.

From: Elegies (Book IV.7)

Cynthia's Ghost

So ghosts do exist: death is not the end of all, and a pale shade vanquishes and escapes the pyre. For I dreamt that Cynthia, who had lately been buried to the drone of the funeral trumpet, was leaning over my bed when after my love's interment sleep hovered over me and I bemoaned the cold empire of my bed. Her hair, her eyes were the same as when she was borne to the grave: her dress was charred at the side, and the fire had gnawed at the familiar beryl on her finger, and Lethe's water had withered her lips. But it was a living voice and spirit that emerged as her brittle fingers cracked with a snap of her thumb:

'Treacherous one, from whom no girl can expect better, can sleep so soon have power over you? Have you so soon forgotten our escapades in the sleepless Subura and my window-sill worn away by nightly guile? How oft by that window did I let down a rope to you and dangle mid-air, descending hand over hand to embrace you? Oft at the crossways we made love, and breast on breast warmed with our passion the road beneath. Alas for the troth you plighted, whose deceitful words the south wind, unwilling to hear, has swept away!

'But no one cried aloud upon my eyes at my passing: I might, had you called me back, have gained another day. No watchman rattled his cleft reed for my sake, and a jagged tile gashed my unprotected head. Besides, who saw you bowed with grief at my funeral or your suit of mourning warmed with tears? If it irked you to accompany the cortege beyond the gates, still you might have bade my bier move more slowly to that point. Why, ungrateful man, did you not call the winds to fan my pyre? Why was my funeral fire not perfumed with spice? Was it then too much to cast hyacinths upon me, no costly gift, and to hallow my grave with wine from a shattered jar?

'Let Lygdamus be tortured, let the branding-iron glow white for that slave: I knew it was his doing, when I drank the wine that foully struck me pale. Though artful Nomas got rid of her secret concoctions, the red-hot brick will declare hers to be guilty hands. She who lately offered herself in public for cheap nights of love now brushes the ground with the gilded hem of her cloak: you did nothing to stop her melting down a gold image of me and putting me to the flames so that she could have a dowry! And she unjustly assigns baskets with heavier loads of wool to any chattering servant who has referred to my beauty; because she placed a bouquet of flowers on my grave, aged Petale is shackled to a foul log of wood; and Lalage is hung by her twisted hair and flogged, because she dared to ask a favour in my name.

'But I chide you not, Propertius, though chiding you deserve: long did I reign supreme in your works. I swear by the rune of the Fates that no man can unravel – as I speak true, so may the three-headed dog bay gently for me – that I kept faith. If I lie, may a hissing viper nest in my grave and brood over my bones.

'For two abodes have been appointed along the foul river, and the whole host rows this way or that. One passage conveys the adulterous Clytemnestra, and carries the Cretan queen whose guile contrived the wooden monstrosity of a cow. But see, the other group are hurried off in a garlanded vessel, where a happy breeze gently fans the roses of Elysium, where sound the strings of melody, Cybele's cymbals, and Lydian lyres struck in the turbaned dance. Andromeda and Hypermnestra, that bride unstained by treachery, tell, glorious heroines, their stories. The one complains that her arms are bruised by chains she suffered through a mother's pride, that her hands deserved not to be fettered to the cold rocks; Hypermnestra tells of the heinous deed dared by her sisters, and how her tears shed in Hades confirm the love we gave on earth: I hide in silence your many sins of infidelity.

'But now I give you instructions, if perchance you are moved, and Chloris' love potions have not utterly bewitched you: let my nurse Parthenie lack nothing in her feeble old age: though she might have done, she showed nogreed towards you; and let not my darling Latris, named for her faithful service, hold up the mirror to another mistress. As for the poems you composed in my honour, burn them, I pray: cease to win praise through me. Plant ivy on my grave, so that its swelling tendrils may bind my delicate bones with intertwining leaves. Where foaming Anio irrigates orchard fields and, by favour of Hercules, ivory never yellows, there on the middle of a pillar inscribe an epitaph worthy of me, but brief, such as the traveller may read as he hastens from Rome:

HERE IN TIBUR'S SOIL LIES GOLDEN CYNTHIA:
FRESH GLORY, ANIO, IS ADDED TO THY BANKS.

'Spurn not the dreams that come through the Righteous Gate: when righteous dreams come, they have the
weight of truth. By night we drift abroad, night frees imprisoned shades, and even Cerberus casts aside his chains, and strays. At dawn the law compels us to return to Lethe's waters: we board,

the ferryman counts the cargo boarded. Other women may possess you now: soon I alone shall hold you: with me you will be, and my bones shall press yours in close entwining.'

When she had thus brought to an end her querulous indictment, the apparition vanished, baffling my embrace.

CHOSEN BY *John Hartley Williams*

JOHN HARTLEY WILLIAMS

The Revenant

We do not die; as ghosts we survive.
    Last night the urn that held her heaped grey ashes
released a spectre. I woke in sweat
    to glimpse above the cold furnace of my bed
the burning gaze of Cynthia herself,
    back from the crematorium, same green eyes,
same dress, but charred, the ring I gave her
    eaten by fire, her lips cracked from searing heat.
A re-born spirit raged in her voice;
    she snapped a soot-encrusted thumb in my face:

'Think you'll ever sleep again? Traitor!
    Remember how you stood beneath my window?
Eagerly down the knotted sheet, I
    slid into your arms and we fucked like tigers
on the ground, waking the whole hostel,
    hollowing out the earth like my window-sill
with climbing out of it, mad for your
    embraces, doing that rope-act to reach you,
swinging there, stupid, on a ripcord.
    My sister nurses heard our every wild sob!'

'The way that hearse reached the cemetery,
    you'd have thought it was a fire truck, me a blaze.
But *you* went no further than the gates.
    In the public viewing room, my casket stood open.

Someone tossed a condom into it,
    then triggered the switch that sent me to the flames
before the priest had droned his prayers?
    You didn't stand guard; don't bother to look shocked.
I know you've no black tie, shoes, suit – but
    wasn't I worth a bunch of discount roses?'

'That bitch Clara, I'm prepared to bet,
    put something in my food, tied my guts in knots.
Haven't you asked yourself what killed me?
    I'm twenty-eight; that's all I'll ever be.
I trust you reach crippled ninety-five.
    Betray Clara for my sake, right across town.
Petal is just waiting to be asked;
    Leila won't say no; Anne is anybody's.
But Clara had the whole football team,
    Sextus, in the shower. How's that make you feel?

'Fact is, lover, I bear you no grudge.
    When people read your poetry, verse is put back
where it belongs, in the world of tears,
    and I'm the one they'll think of when things go wrong.
Let cockroaches couple on this vase
    and hatch their children to grow fat off my ash
if I've ever said less than the truth.
    I was always yours. I never wavered once
although your friends were always trying
    to climb in my bed, do you a favour. Ha!'

'Let Clara change the décor, Sextus,
    and paint me out of your life. Employ another
housekeeper, but give old Julia
    a pension till she dies. Please see her all right;
don't make her work for your monstrous friends.
    Stop writing verses; Clara couldn't care less.
Conquer your loathing of the graveyard
    and plant beneath the marble slab with my name
– on which I hope you'll write an epitaph –
    a dog-rose you've stolen from a city park.'

'Or kick out that whore. Leave town for good.
    Abandon your thuggish friends. London's a prison.
The river still feeds the meadows where
    we built that crazy tower near our village.
Clear away the ivy tangled round
    the base and engrave this above my ashes:
IN THIS RANK ORCHARD LIES CYNTHIA
ONLY SEXTUS KNOWS WHAT SHE WAS LIKE.
Damsons droop their crimson clusters there
    and weigh down the boughs gently to touch your head.
Let the cursive of your pen find thought.
    Feel the life return that made you write for me.'

'Ah, perhaps you won't. She'll not let go.
   But I'm there inside you, deeper than she knows.
Night has released me into your brain;
   the coming of dawn compels me to go back.
Clara can have you for now, but soon
   I'll reclaim you, Sextus – our dust will mingle.
Think you're dreaming? Don't you know my voice?
   How often have I whispered from the darkness?'
She spoke. And when she was done, I reached
with both arms up for her. Straightway, she vanished.

ANNA AKHMATOVA

translated from Russian by Stanley Kunitz and Max Hayward

The Last Toast

I drink to our ruined house,
to the dolor of my life
to our loneliness together;
and to you I raise my glass,
to lying lips that have betrayed us,
to dead-cold, pitiless eyes,
and to the hard realities:
that the world is brutal and coarse,
that God in fact has not saved us.

CHOSEN BY *Elaine Feinstein*

Another Toast

She drinks to her ruined home.
My own is not destroyed.
Still, the loneliness in marriage
is something I can toast.
I drink to your hostile stare,
our quarrels, your infidelity,
and what you resented most:
that God did not choose to save you,
and took some pity on me.

D. H. LAWRENCE

To Women, As Far As I'm Concerned

The feelings I don't have, I don't have.
The feelings I don't have, I won't say I have.
The feelings you say you have, you don't have.
The feelings you would like us both to have, we neither of us
    have.

The feelings people ought to have, they never have.
If people say they've got feelings, you may be pretty sure they
    haven't got them.

So if you want either of us to feel anything at all
you'd better abandon all idea of feelings altogether.

CHOSEN BY *Jean Sprackland*

JEAN SPRACKLAND

Feelings

He adjusted the chain on my bike, so I let him
leave a few oily marks on my blouse. After that

he'd always be coming round when my parents were out,
asking how did I feel. Had my feelings
grown, altered or faded. Were they dying.

I thought of a tortoise asleep in a box of straw.
In spring you had to reach in and feel for warmth,
carry it onto the grass and try it with dandelions.

It was weeks before I knew that all I wanted
was to be driven at night up to the gravel pit
wearing only his proper coat, then to throw it off
and run into the water feeling nothing at all.

CHARLOTTE MEW

On the Road to the Sea

We passed each other, turned and stopped for half an hour, then went
our way,
    I who make other women smile did not make you—
But no man can move mountains in a day.
    So this hard thing is yet to do.

But first I want your life:—before I die I want to see
    The world that lies behind the strangeness of your eyes,
There is nothing gay or green there for my gathering, it may be,
       Yet on brown fields there lies
A haunting purple bloom: is there not something in grey skies
         And in grey sea?
    I want what world there is behind your eyes,
    I want your life and you will not give it me.

  Now, if I look, I see you walking down the years,
    Young, and through August fields—a face, a thought,—
         a swinging dream perched on a stile—;
    I would have liked (so vile we are!) to have taught you tears
        But most to have made you smile.

      To-day is not enough or yesterday: God sees it all—
Your length on sunny lawns, the wakeful rainy nights—; tell me—;
    (how vain to ask),
    but it is not a question—just a call—;
Show me, then, only your notched inches climbing up the garden wall,
        I like you best when you are small.

        Is this a stupid thing to say
        Not having spent with you one day?
    No matter; I shall never touch your hair
    Or hear the little tick behind your breast,
        Still it is there,
        And as a flying bird
Brushes the branches where it may not rest

                    I have brushed your hand and heard
The child in you: I like that best.

So small, so dark, so sweet: and were you also then too grave and wise?
        Always I think. Then put your far off little hand in mine; – Oh! let it rest;
I will not stare into the early world beyond the opening eyes,
        Or vex or scare what I love best.

        But I want your life before mine bleeds away—
            Here—not in heavenly hereafters—soon,—
            I want your smile this very afternoon,
        (The last of all my vices, pleasant people used to say,
            I wanted and I sometimes got – the Moon!)

            You know, at dusk, the last bird's cry,
        And round the house the flap of the bat's low flight,
            Trees that go black against the sky
        And then—how soon the night!

        No shadow of you on any bright road again,
And at the darkening end of this – what voice? whose kiss? As if you'd say!
It is not I who have walked with you, it will not be I who take away
        Peace, peace, my little handful of the gleaner's grain
        From your reaped fields at the shut of day.

                Peace! Would you not rather die
            Reeling,—with all the cannons at your ear?
                So, at least, would I,
            And I may not be here
            To-night, to-morrow morning or next year.
            Still, I will let you keep your life a little while,
                    See dear
        I have made you smile.

CHOSEN BY *Jane Weir*

JANE WEIR

I'm Trying to Make Gnocchi di Patate for Angelina for Old Time's Sake

When the potato puree's dry
enough I add the flour, butter, eggs,
season well, knead to a dough.
One thing I forgot to say –
that many times I had to
brush your bronzed hands away,
as you tried to play
scales over me.

No different from that day
we found those shadows
lounging in the dusky
corner of a fifteenth century chapel,
and slim your fingers picked
and unpicked like an inquisition
at the hook and eye
of my bra strap,
until it broke free, flew,
askew like a bat
and my breasts
soared from the cartilage
curves of its satin uplift . . .

I banished you with the civet
to the other end of the island.
From afar I let you gaze towards a star,
as I roll and cut small cylinders,
that in turn become dimpled crescents,
like the spores underneath
an up-turned fern leaf.

I drop each crescent one by one,
while grinning you heat the plate.
Both of us now are drinking Chianti.
It takes about three minutes
I know because I've learnt to gauge –
like all good cooks do.

I serve it simple
in the Genoese way –
with pesto.
Flushed, a loose
strand or two straying,
I sit across the table
and pass you the fork,
the swooning plate.
For your Mother's sake
stop looking at me
that way – start eating.

JOHN DONNE

Elegie: To his Mistress Going To Bed

Come, Madam, come, all rest my powers defie,
Until I labour, I in labour lye.
The foe oft-times, having the foe in sight,
Is tir'd with standing, though they never fight.
Off with that girdle, like heavens zone glistering
But a farre fairer world encompassing.
Unpin that spangled brest-plate, which you weare
That th'eyes of busy fooles may be stopt there:
Unlace your selfe, for that harmonious chime
Tells me from you that now 'tis your bed time.
Off with that happy buske, whom I envye
That still can be, and still can stand so nigh.
Your gownes going off such beauteous state reveales
As when from flowery meads th'hills shadow steals.
Off with your wyrie coronet and showe
The hairy dyadem which on you doth growe.
Off with those shoes: and then safely tread
In this loves hallow'd temple, this soft bed.
In such white robes heavens Angels us'd to bee
Receiv'd by men; Thou Angel bring'st with thee
A heaven like Mahomets Paradise; and though
Ill spirits walk in white, we easily know
By this these Angels from an evil sprite:
They set our haires, but these the flesh upright.
　　Licence my roving hands, and let them goe
Behind, before, above, between, below.
Oh my America, my new found lande,
My kingdome, safeliest when with one man man'd,
My myne of precious stones, my Empiree,
How blest am I in this discovering thee.

To enter in these bonds is to be free,
Then where my hand is set my seal shall be.
    Full nakedness, all joyes are due to thee.
As soules unbodied, bodies uncloth'd must bee
To taste whole joyes. Gems which you women use
Are as Atlanta's balls, cast in mens viewes,
That when a fooles eye lighteth on a gem
His earthly soule may covet theirs not them.
Like pictures, or like bookes gay coverings made
For laymen, are all women thus arraid;
Themselves are mystique bookes, which only wee
Whom their imputed grace will dignify
Must see reveal'd. Then since I may knowe,
As liberally as to a midwife showe
Thy selfe; cast all, yea this white linnen hence.
Here is no penance, much lesse innocence.
    To teach thee, I am naked first: Why then
What need'st thou have more covering than a man.

CHOSEN BY *Owen Sheers*

OWEN SHEERS

Elegy: To Her Husband Going To Bed

'Come, madam, come' you say, all voice from where you lie,
hidden, so for us both our ears must serve as eyes.
Thus divided, you within our curtained bed,
myself without, paused at the break and half undressed,
we are as two blind beggars robbed of sight
with no more than sound imagination to shed light
upon the other's face, posture, skin,
until I enter and, allowing you the same, we'll begin.
   One sense denied the others grow; the mind anticipation is,
but unlike yours, sir, waiting cat-like on the minutes,
mine is watchful for the months beyond. For has not our union
undone four times already the very lives we had begun?
Four times two skulls have grown within my womb,
four times have I mothered a child into a tomb,
and four times we two, becoming one, have condemned not saved,
our performance no more than as midwives for the grave.
   'As heaven's Angel' you say on the falling of my dress.
Thy wit is sharp, sir, but how long before we give your image flesh?
Then only in your dreams will I come here to visit you,
unclad not just of this, my dress, but of my body too.
And yet, knowing with my body I may be laying down my life,
still I part this curtain, take my position as your wife.
For what is life which life does not make? What a curtain
                                                  without a bed?
What a ring without a finger? What a marriage without being wed?
Life must be lived or else the reaper reaps all,
so our nakedness is no sheathing of a sword
but rather a storming of his dark citadel,

for which, removing my breast plate, your shirt, we are armoured
   well.
'Tis just as you have preached, sir, (though truer than you

can see):
'To enter in these bonds is to be free.'
In truth though, on this battlefield you but play the man;
'tis left to me, your wife, to make the final stand.
For though we set out to vanquish death together,
'tis I, in this fight, who am the truer soldier.
Your part, though vital, is simple; finished before it's begun –
what more needst thou than the covering of a woman?
For me, however, my duty is still borne
long after you've slept and risen to meet the morn.
Your sword unsheathed, your labour and part are done.
Mine, my lord, will have only just begun.

Note: Ann More married John Donne when she was sixteen years
old. During the sixteen years of their marriage she bore her
husband twelve children of which only seven survived. She died in
childbirth at the age of thirty-two. John Donne never remarried.

PHILIP LARKIN

Home Is So Sad

Home is so sad. It stays as it was left,
Shaped to the comfort of the last to go
As if to win them back. Instead, bereft
Of anyone to please, it withers so,
Having no heart to put aside the theft

And turn again to what it started as,
A joyous shot at how things ought to be,
Long fallen wide. You can see how it was:
Look at the pictures and the cutlery.
The music in the piano stool. That vase.

CHOSEN BY *Vicki Feaver*

VICKI FEAVER

Home Is Here Now

Home is here, now
at this table with its gouged
and scratched wood
where I peel an orange,
the spray from the zest
sending shivers up my nose.

I can see my hands' blue veins
and swollen red knuckles,
and the diamond highlight
on the blade of my knife,
and bright rind falling
in a long curl.

It's the quiet time
at the end of the day:
no birdsong, no wind;
just my in and out breaths
and the faint tearing
of pith parting from flesh.

CHRISTINA ROSSETTI

The One Certainty

Vanity of vanities, the Preacher saith,
　　All things are vanity. The eye and ear
　　Cannot be filled with what they see and hear.
Like early dew, or like the sudden breath
Of wind, or like the grass that withereth,
　　Is man, tossed to and fro by hope and fear:
　　So little joy hath he, so little cheer,
Till all things end in the long dust of death.
To-day is still the same as yesterday,
　　To-morrow also even as one of them;
And there is nothing new under the sun:
Until the ancient race of Time be run,
　　The old thorns shall grow out of the old stem,
And morning shall be cold and twilight grey.

CHOSEN BY *Jane Feaver*

JANE FEAVER

Housekeeping

Sometimes you might hear us
like Adam and Eve berating each other
argument, recrimination, who does what . . .

I inspect her room when she's away
and can't deny it bears a close resemblance
to my own – strewn, disarrayed – a clutch of cups,
each with its flowery eiderdown of mould.
Her doll's house is a cupboard
for pencil sharpenings, sweet wrappers, half-eaten biscuits,
a honey-trap – how many times has she been told? –
for the mice and spiders clamouring in the wings.

Dithering, where to begin, I alight
on an old reading book she has of mine,
Helping at Home. How things change –
the mother splendid in her pearls
the daughter pinnied and delightfully behaved,
'I am helping mummy to dust.'

Why, when I detest this business,
am I so hell bent on inducting her,
as if it were part of our DNA
the be-all and end all of the species?
What other animal is so enslaved?

Sometimes you might see us,
all quarrelling spent, pressed to the glass,
the greenness outside – no apron
in sight, no obscene yellow glove – a world
from which we have been barred,
self-cleaning, miraculously bright,
before history, before dust.

LUCILLE CLIFTON

the lost baby poem

the time i dropped your almost body down
down to meet the waters under the city
and run one with the sewage into the sea
what did i know about waters rushing back
what did i know about drowning
or being drowned

you would have been born into winter
in the year of the disconnected gas
and no car   we would have made the thin
walk over Genesee hill into the Canada wind
to watch you slip like ice into strangers' hands
you would have fallen naked as snow into winter
if you were here i could tell you these
and some other things

if i am ever less than a mountain
for your definite brothers and sisters
let the rivers pour over my head
let the seas take me for a spiller
of seas   let black men call me stranger
always   for your never named sake

CHOSEN BY *Clare Shaw*

CLARE SHAW

The No Baby Poem

There will be no ceremony
in a quiet wood for this. Today
the sun does not matter.
You have simply not made it
into existence. All science, all alchemy
have failed from the start.
There is only this
injury, nameless and wet.

You are everything I know now
of loss, the perfect
grey weight of it, constant,
which has turned down the light
in my face.

Had just one moment
of one month been different,
you would have been born
into winter.
We would have made the drive
in the late afternoon,
past front rooms in Luddenden
yellow with warmth
a jewellery of light in each window
to see you erupt like summer
into our hands.

No-show, non-event,
we have lost you
to a world where there is no word,
even for absence.
Whatever could have made you
is irrelevant. Today,
the slightest breeze could blow me
clean away.

YEHUDA AMICHAI

Ibn Gabirol

Could be a wound leaking,
could be a poem sung.

Always something is flashed open,
always there is pain.

My dad was a tree in a forest of dads
concealed under green mould.

O widows of flesh, orphans of blood!
I need to escape.

Eyes sharp like a can-opener
opened heavy secrets.

But because of the pain in my life
God is able to see into the world,

I am the door
to his rooms.

CHOSEN AND TRANSLATED BY *David Hart*
(with thanks to Riki Jackson, who talked the poem
through from the Hebrew)

DAVID HART

Yehuda Amichai

I have from the Internet
a photo of your chair,
neither you nor words
nor God is there.

What else to write
in a time of distress
but of the Most High's
tidal sadness?

The child builds a temple of sand
and another and another
is taken by the flood tide.

God sharing an ambulance
has been taken out,
with whom can I bargain now
for light?

Who will purpose me
to know the plan?
Can I bargain
with a loud Welsh Amen?

My lips have not been licked
by enough earth spit.

God enters my wound,
bathes in the pus
and will find
only a poem there.

GERARD MANLEY HOPKINS

Pied Beauty

Glory be to God for dappled things –
    For skies of couple-colour as a brinded cow;
        For rose-moles all in stipple upon trout that swim;
Fresh-firecoal chestnut-falls; finches' wings;
    Landscape plotted and pieced-fold, fallow, and plough;
        And áll trádes, their gear and tackle and trim.

All things counter, original, spare, strange;
    Whatever is fickle, freckled (who knows how?)
        With swift, slow; sweet, sour; adazzle, dim;
He fathers-forth whose beauty is past change:
        Praise him.

CHOSEN BY *Michael Woods*

MICHAEL WOODS

A Bluebell from St Beuno's

Weary after a long term we drove to Wales –
your world for a while where *springs not fail*.
After the study session at the Bod Eryn Hotel
we tucked into pied beauty for lunch –
trout and almonds, chips with a twist of lemon.
We traced our way over your pastoral forehead,
the turrets of St Beuno's set square
against the Vale of Clwyd.

Not the right thing to do, perhaps,
but I picked a flower that went to press.
What you might have said to me about
my act of stealth as I slipped the bluebell
between the passions of your poems
I know I'll never know but, since then,
veins have been visibly bound, fastened
to a page that's almost the colour of flesh.

The Lemons

Listen to me, the poets laureate
walk only among plants
with rare names: boxwood, privet and acanthus.
But I like roads that lead to grassy
ditches where boys
scoop up a few starved
eels out of half-dry puddles:
paths that run along the banks
come down among the tufted canes
and end in orchards, among the lemon trees.

Better if the hubbub of the birds
dies out, swallowed by the blue:
we can hear more of the whispering
of friendly branches in not-quite-quiet air,
and the sensations of this smell
that can't divorce itself from earth
and rains a restless sweetness on the heart.
Here, by some miracle, the war
of troubled passions calls a truce;
here we poor, too, receive our share of riches,
which is the fragrance of the lemons.

See, in these silences where things
give over and seem on the verge of betraying
their final secret,
sometimes we feel we're about
to uncover an error in Nature,
the still point of the world, the link that won't hold,
the thread to untangle that will finally lead
to the heart of a truth.

The eye scans its surroundings,
the mind inquires aligns divides
in the perfume that gets diffused
at the day's most languid.
It's in these silences you see
in every fleeting human
shadow some disturbed Divinity.

But the illusion fails, and time returns us
to noisy cities where the blue
is seen in patches, up between the roofs.
The rain exhausts the earth then;
winter's tedium weighs the houses down,
the light turns miserly – the soul bitter.
Till one day through a half-shut gate
in a courtyard, there among the trees,
we can see the yellow of the lemons;
and the chill in the heart
melts, and deep in us
the golden horns of sunlight
pelt their songs.

CHOSEN BY *Roger Garfitt*

Harebell

Almost bare of blue,

a blown egg
of colour,

a shell sculling

on the tide-race
of air,

it catches you

unawares, an after-
image that floats up

out of nowhere,

doubling you back
in disbelief

to the sheen of ice

or honesty, the petals
fluted in Gothic plate

and the silicate

of blue there is no
imagining,

a breath taken

from the thin soils
of the edge,

a semitone

the earth, crouched
over its elbow pipes,

has wrestled clear.

Pangur Ban

I and Pangur Ban my cat,
'Tis a like task we are at:
Hunting mice is his delight,
Hunting words I sit all night.

Better far than praise of men
'Tis to sit with book and pen;
Pangur bears me no ill-will,
He too plies his simple skill.

'Tis a merry task to see
At our tasks how glad are we,
When at home we sit and find
Entertainment to our mind.

Oftentimes a mouse will stray
In the hero Pangur's way;
Oftentimes my keen thought set
Takes a meaning in its net.

'Gainst the wall he sets his eye
Full and fierce and sharp and sly;
'Gainst the wall of knowledge I
All my little wisdom try.

When a mouse darts from its den,
O how glad is Pangur then!
O what gladness do I prove
When I solve the doubts I love!

So in peace our task we ply,
Pangur Ban, my cat, and I;
In our arts we find our bliss,
I have mine and he has his.

Practice every day has made
Pangur perfect in his trade;
I get wisdom day and night
Turning darkness into light.

CHOSEN BY *Michael Schmidt*

Pangur Bàn

i.

Jerome has his enormous dozy lion.
Myself, I have a cat, my Pangur Bàn.

What did Jerome feed up his lion with?
Always he's fat and fleecy, always sleeping

As if after a meal. Perhaps a Christian?
Perhaps a lamb, or a fish, or a loaf of bread.

His lion's always smiling, chin on paw,
What looks like purring rippling his face

And there on Jerome's escritoire by the quill and ink pot
The long black thorn he drew from the lion's paw.

Look, Pangur, at the picture of the lion –
Not a mouser like you, not lean, not ever

Chasing a quill as it flutters over parchment
Leaving its trail that is the word of God.

Pangur, you are so trim beside the lion.
– Unlike Jerome in the mouth of his desert cave

Wrapped in a wardrobe of robes despite the heat,
I in this Irish winter, Pangur Bàn,

Am cold, without so much as your pillow case
Of fur, white, with ginger tips on ears and tail.

ii.

My name is neither here nor there, I am employed
By Colum Cille who will be a saint

Because of me and how I have set down
The word of God. He pays. He goes to heaven.

I stay on earth, in this cell with the high empty window,
The long light in summer, the winter stars.

I work with my quill and colours, bent and blinder
Each season, colder, but the pages fill.

Just when I started work the cat arrived
Sleek and sharp at my elbow, out of nowhere;

I dipped my pen. He settled in with me.
He listened and replied. He kept my counsel.

iii.

Here in the margin, Pangur, I inscribe you.
Almost Amen. Prowl out of now and go down

Into time's garden, wary with your tip-toe hearing.
You'll live well enough on mice and shrews till you find

The next scriptorium, a bowl of milk. Some scribe
Will recognise you, Pangur Bàn, and feed you;

You'll find your way to him as you did to me
From nowhere (but you sniffed out your Jerome).

Stay by him, too, until his Gospel's done.
(I linger over John, the closing verses,

You're restless, won't be touched. I'm old. The solstice.)
Amen, dear Pangur Bàn. Amen. Be sly.

EMILY DICKINSON

'Grief is a Mouse'

Grief is a Mouse —
And chooses Wainscot in the Breast
For his Shy House —
And baffles quest —

Grief is a Thief — quick startled —
Pricks His Ear — report to hear
Of that Vast Dark —
That swept His Being — back —

Grief is a Juggler — boldest at the Play —
Lest if He flinch — the eye that way
Pounce on His Bruises — One — say — or - Three —
Grief is a Gourmand — spare His luxury —

Best Grief is Tongueless — before He'll tell —
Burn Him in the Public Square —
His Ashes — will
Possibly — if they refuse — How then know —
Since a Rack couldn't coax a syllable — now.

CHOSEN BY *Penelope Shuttle*

Grief x 2

1. Keeper

He's the keeper of my wardrobe,
repairs my coat of shining mail,
warms my iron slippers,
wraps me all winter in a leaden cloak

Wherever I travel,
he packs my bronze gowns,
blue-steel shellsuit and copper cardigan,
garments forged not sewn

Only Grief is strong enough
to lug my suitcase out to the car –
Surely, he says,
you will not go naked?

2. On his Shoulders

As always Grief turns away,
because I have too-sorrow a heart

Nowadays
I have neither sun nor moon,
and weep for hours, like Pyotr Illych,

because Grief no longer carries me
on his broad shoulders,

but takes ship for Mecca,
not caring if I suffer for days,
like a woman in old-fashioned childbed,

or a far-north river
taking ten months of the year to wake up,

autumn
hoping against hope to be spring
or *Summer making her light escape* . . .

PATRICK KAVANAGH

The Hospital

A year ago I fell in love with the functional ward
Of a chest hospital: square cubicles in a row,
Plain concrete, wash basins – an art lover's woe,
Not counting how the fellow in the next bed snored.
But nothing whatever is by love debarred,
The common and banal her heat can know.
The corridor led to a stairway and below
Was the inexhaustible adventure of a gravelled yard.

This is what love does to things: the Rialto Bridge,
The main gate that was bent by a heavy lorry,
The seat at the back of a shed that was a suntrap.
Naming these things is the love-act and its pledge;
For we must record love's mystery without claptrap,
Snatch out of time the passionate transitory.

CHOSEN BY *Paul Henry*

PAUL HENRY

The Waiting Room

An empty coatstand in a public building, in August.
Even this is draped with your absence.
The rags of a seagull's cry hang from it now.

Nothing is devoid of love.
How many years did I waste, listening out
for your voice?

          The park through a window,
swollen with leaves, smothers its coatstands well.

Thin veils of clouds, a city's prayers,
fall away to the west. For a split second
I can see your eyes.

          But if I break my gaze
the gull has slipped its hook, the sea
is a long way away.

ELIZABETH BISHOP

One Art

The art of losing isn't hard to master;
so many things seem filled with the intent
to be lost that their loss is no disaster.

Lose something every day. Accept the fluster
of lost door keys, the hour badly spent.
The art of losing isn't hard to master.

Then practice losing farther, losing faster:
places, and names, and where it was you meant
to travel. None of these will bring disaster.

I lost my mother's watch. And look! my last, or
next-to-last, of three loved houses went.
The art of losing isn't hard to master.

I lost two cities, lovely ones. And, vaster,
some realms I owned, two rivers, a continent.
I miss them, but it wasn't a disaster.

—Even losing you (the joking voice, a gesture
I love) I shan't have lied. It's evident
the art of losing's not too hard to master
though it may look like (*Write* it!) like disaster.

CHOSEN BY *Paula Meehan*

PAULA MEEHAN

Quitting the Bars

Quitting's hard but staying sober's harder.
The day by day; the drudge and boredom bit;
not sure if the self is cell or warder.

You quit the bars; you quit the sordid ardour;
you quit the tulpas sucking on your tit.
Quitting's hard but staying sober's harder.

You sometimes think you got away with murder.
The shady souls regard you as you sit –
you wonder if they are wards or warders

in this sad café. The mind's last border
dissolves. Guilt has done a midnight flit.
Quitting's hard but staying sober's harder.

So sip cool water; the light's a wonder
streaming out in wave-particles. You've lit
up bright your prison cell. Body – warder

of your dreams – will be the dreams' recorder,
though wrapped now in a skin that doesn't fit.
Quitting's hard but staying sober's harder;
stranger for you being both ward and warder.

MURIEL RUKEYSER

Poem

I lived in the first century of world wars.
Most mornings I would be more or less insane,
The newspapers would arrive with their careless stories,
The news would pour out of various devices
Interrupted by attempts to sell products to the unseen.
I would call my friends on other devices;
They would be more or less mad for similar reasons.
Slowly I would get to pen and paper,
Make my poems for others unseen and unborn.
In the day I would be reminded of those men and women
Brave, setting up signals across vast distances,
Considering a nameless way of living, of almost unimagined
    values.
As the lights darkened, as the light of night brightened,
We would try to imagine them, try to find each other.
To construct peace, to make love, to reconcile
Waking with sleeping, ourselves with each other,
Ourselves with ourselves. We would try by any means
To reach the limits of ourselves, to reach beyond ourselves,
To let go the means, to wake.

I lived in the first century of these wars.

CHOSEN BY *Linda Chase*

LINDA CHASE

Waking

to Muriel Rukeyser

That day, when you woke up more or less insane,
might have been my wedding day, December 1967.
My mother, born when you were born, woke up too
in New York City, reaching for her Phenobarbital,
fretting – her new son-in-law was too radical, too smart.
(His parents, after all, German Jewish Communists,
were both suspected spies!) In light of this, she fears
the wedding toasts could be unsafe, precarious –
then remembers, no, Immigration barred these un-Americans.
Still, the guest list on the bridegroom's side
looked like something blacker than Joe McCarthy's list.
My parents' swish apartment, like the newsroom of a war,
is sealed off as taxi tyres slap the street and horses' hooves
percuss the fumes beside the entrance to the park.
From here, oh yes, we're central; ahead the distance spreads
out towards the second century of these wars.
My mother masks herself with glasses, fumbles for a pen and writes,

'chill champagne, pay doorman, check the seating plan.'

W. H. AUDEN

Refugee Blues

Say this city has ten million souls,
Some are living in mansions, some are living in holes:
Yet there's no place for us, my dear, yet there's no place for us.

Once we had a country and we thought it fair,
Look in the atlas and you'll find it there:
We cannot go there now, my dear, we cannot go there now.

In the village churchyard there grows an old yew,
Every spring it blossoms anew:
Old passports can't do that, my dear, old passports can't do that.

The consul banged the table and said:
'If you've got no passport you're officially dead':
But we are still alive, my dear, but we are still alive.

Went to a committee; they offered me a chair;
Asked me politely to return next year:
But where shall we go today, my dear, but where shall we go today?

Came to a public meeting; the speaker got up and said:
'If we let them in, they will steal our daily bread';
He was talking of you and me, my dear, he was talking of you and
     me.

Thought I heard the thunder rumbling in the sky;
It was Hitler over Europe, saying: They must die',
O we were in his mind, my dear, O we were in his mind.

Saw a poodle in a jacket fastened with a pin,
Saw a door opened and a cat let in:
But they weren't German Jews, my dear, but they weren't German
Jews.

Went down to the harbour and stood upon the quay,
Saw the fish swimming as if they were free:
Only ten feet away, my dear, only ten feet away.

Walked through a wood, saw the birds in the trees;
They had no politicians and sang at their ease:
They weren't the human race, my dear, they weren't the human
race.

Dreamed I saw a building with a thousand floors,
A thousand windows and a thousand doors;
Not one of them was ours, my dear, not one of them was ours.

Stood on a great plain in the falling snow;
Ten thousand soldiers marched to and fro:
Looking for you and me, my dear, looking for you and me.

CHOSEN BY *Robert Minhinnick*

The Yellow Palm

As I made my way down Palestine Street
I watched a funeral pass –
all the women waving lilac stems
around a coffin made of glass
and the face of the man who lay within
who had breathed a poison gas.

As I made my way down Palestine Street
I heard the call to prayer
and I stopped at the door of the golden mosque
to watch the faithful there
but there was blood on the walls and muezzin's eyes
were wild with his despair.

As I made my way down Palestine Street
I met two blind beggars
and into their hands I pressed my hands
with a hundred black dinars;
and their salutes were those of Imperial Guard
in the Mother of all Wars.

As I made my way down Palestine Street
I smelled the wide Tigris,
the river smell that lifts the air
in a city such as this;
but down on my head fell the barbarian sun
that knows no armistice.

As I made my way down Palestine Street
I saw a cruise missile,
a slow and silver caravan
on its slow and silver mile,
and a beggar child turned up his face
and blessed it with a smile.

As I made my way down Palestine Street
under the yellow palms
I saw their branches hung with yellow dates
all sweeter than salaams,
and when that same child reached up to touch,
the fruit fell in his arms.

BEN JONSON

Echo's Song

Slow, slow, fresh fount, keepe time with my salt teares;
Yet slower, yet, O faintly gentle springs:
List to the heavy part the musique beares,
      Woe weepes out her division, when she sings.
      Droupe hearbs, and flowres;
      Fall griefe in showres;
      Our beauties are not ours:
               O, I could still
(Like melting snow upon some craggie hill,)
      drop, drop, drop, drop,
Since natures pride is, now, a wither'd daffodill.

CHOSEN BY *Craig Raine*

CRAIG RAINE

Marcel's Fancy Dress Party

For Jan Eijkelboom,
Poet and Translator on his Eightieth Birthday 1 March 2006

'Au premier moment je ne compris pas pourquoi j'hésitais à
reconnaître le maître de maison, les invités, et pourquoi chacun
semblait s'être «fait une tête», génerallement poudrée et qui les
changeait complétement.' Proust: *Le temps retrouvé*

When we floss our teeth
we look like Francis Bacon's
screaming Popes.

How does it feel, Jan,
to be translated –
so quickly, so brilliantly,

so unfaithfully,
into old age?
Into this convincing,

irresistibly plausible
eighty-year-old
everyone is persuaded by?

That seems to everyone original.
Not a version, not an imitation,
not approximate at all.

Only two minutes ago,
you were so young and biological
you were hardly you.

You were biology itself.
Even now you are exactly the same,
you feel exactly the same,

but you are different.
Your body speaks another language
you don't quite understand.

You have the rudiments.
But it isn't fluent.
                    You wonder,

is it possible to flirt
in this foreign language?
Is it possible to write

another kind of poetry,
awkward in your mouth,
where you might welcome want?

And you wait, patiently,
still with your full head of hair,
for the electric toothbrush

to reach its reliable shudder
of happiness – infallible
in your fallible hand.

'Death will come and will have your eyes . . .'

Death will come and will have your eyes –
this death that accompanies us
from morning till evening, unsleeping,
deaf, like an old remorse
or an absurd vice. Your eyes
will be a useless word,
a suppressed cry, a silence.
That's what you see each morning
when alone with yourself you lean
toward the mirror. O precious hope,
that day we too will know
that you are life and you are nothingness.

Death has a look for everyone.
Death will come and will have your eyes.
It will be like renouncing a vice,
like seeing a dead face
reappear in the mirror,
like listening to a lip that's shut.
We'll go down into the maelstrom mute.

CHOSEN BY *Dennis O'Driscoll*

Towards A Cesare Pavese Title

(*Verrà la Morte e Avrà i Tuoi Occhi*)

Death will come and it will wear your eyes.

Death demands the handover of your eyes.

Death eyes you, stares you in the face.

Then death assumes the running of your eyes.

Death powders cheeks, shadows eyes.

Death would take the eyes out of your head.

Death will seize your assets, cut off your eye supply.

Death lashes out at your defenceless eyes.

You are up to your eyes in death.

Death takes after you, eyes the image of yours.

You would recognise death with your eyes shut.

Death will give you dagger glances, evil eyes.

Death makes eye contact at last.

Death will come and it will steal your looks.

If

If you can keep your head when all about you
Are losing theirs and blaming it on you,
If you can trust yourself when all men doubt you,
But make allowance for their doubting too;
If you can wait and not be tired by waiting,
Or being lied about, don't deal in lies,
Or being hated, don't give way to hating,
And yet don't look too good, nor talk too wise:

If you can dream – and not make dreams your master;
If you can think – and not make thoughts your aim;
If you can meet with Triumph and Disaster
And treat those two impostors just the same;
If you can bear to hear the truth you've spoken
Twisted by knaves to make a trap for fools,
Or watch the things you gave your life to, broken,
And stoop and build 'em up with worn-out tools:

If you can make one heap of all your winnings
And risk it on one turn of pitch-and-toss,
And lose, and start again at your beginnings
And never breathe a word about your loss;
If you can force your heart and nerve and sinew
To serve your turn long after they are gone,
And so hold on when there is nothing in you
Except the Will which says to them: 'Hold on!'

If you can talk with crowds and keep your virtue,
Or walk with Kings – nor lose the common touch.
If neither foes nor loving friends can hurt you,
If all men count with you, but none too much;

If you can fill the unforgiving minute
With sixty seconds' worth of distance run,
Yours is the Earth and everything that's in it,
And – which is more – you'll be a Man, my son!

CHOSEN BY *Carol Ann Duffy*

Kipling

The base of the heap was the profit made
on the sale of his house,
the mortgage paid and the balance saved
in well-thumbed dosh. On top of that
went the wad dished out by the dude in the hotel bar
who purchased the car, plus the loot from the little guy
who fancied the wife's Diane. The kids' four bikes
went in a weekend job-lot sale
to a priest from Wales, no questions asked,
hard cash, and the caravan to a melancholy man
with a van and a female twin and a tin
of fifty-pound notes. The heap grew,
but he knew what he knew, had a tip
on a cert that would hit pay-dirt
and he needed more. The art on the walls
made seven grand and the timeshare pad in Portugal
raised seven again. The dog was a bitch,
never been snipped, a pedigree who was ripe
for pups, so that put her price up.
He flogged the pension plan to a middleman
from Milton Keynes, plus the unit trusts,
and tossed the stinking tax-free stuff
on the heap. A pawnbroker gave a not-bad price
for his watch, pen, lighter, cufflinks, ID chain, and the wife's
engagement ring fetched as much again on its tod.
A car-boot sale from the back of a cab
took care of his clothes, five suits, three pairs
of boots, a dozen shirts, fifteen jazzy ties.
The children's toys walked out at a fiver each
from a cardboard box and the videos vanished,

hand over fist to the first in line with a 50p piece.
Ditto, at double the cost and a snip at the price,
over a thousand CDs. Beatles. Bee Gees. Byrds. He peddled
the dodgy plants from the potting-shed,
dried in polythene bags, to the local youth
and shifted enough to score a sniff of the harder stuff
for himself. The heap was massive, huge,
so he hawked his arse six times round the park
to top it off, icing the cake, then hired a skip to lug it round
to the betting-shop and had it counted, twice,
while he wrote out his betting-slip with a sawn-off pen.
Kipling to win. Uttoxeter. 3.10. After the off, horse riderless
and jockey tossed, he never breathed a word about his loss.

Acknowledgements

The editor and publishers wish to thank the following for permission to use copyright material:

Anna Akhmatova – 'The Last Toast' from *Poems of Akhmatova* translated by Stanley Kunitz and Max Hayward, published by Harvill. Reprinted by permission of The Random House Group Ltd.

Yehuda Amichai – 'Ibn Gabirol' translated by David Hart with thanks to Riki Jackson, by permission of the translator.

W. H. Auden – 'Musée des Beaux Arts', by permission of Faber and Faber Ltd and Curtis Brown Ltd. 'Refugee Blues' by permission of Faber and Faber Ltd and Curtis Brown Ltd.

Elizabeth Bishop – 'Insomnia' and 'One Art' from *The Complete Poems 1927–1979* by Elizabeth Bishop, by permission of Farrar, Straus and Giroux, LLC.

C. P. Cavafy – 'Ithaka' by C. P. Cavafy, translated by Edmund Keeley and Philip Sherrard, by permission of Rogers, Coleridge & White.

Joseph P. Clanchy – 'The Clock' by Dafydd Ap Gwilym translated by Joseph P. Clanchy, by permission of the translator.

Lucille Clifton – 'the lost baby poem' from *Good Woman: Poems and a Memoir 1969–1980*. Copyright © 1987 by Lucille Clifton. Reprinted with the permission of BOA Editions, Ltd., www.boaeditions.org.

Walter de la Mare – 'Echo' from *The Complete Poems of Walter de la Mare* (1975), by permission of The Literary Trustees of Walter de la Mare and the Society of Authors as their representative.

Imtiaz Dharker – 'Myth' from *The Terrorist at My Table* (Bloodaxe Books, 2006), by permission of Bloodaxe Books.

Allen Ginsberg – 'Howl' from *Allen Ginsberg: Selected Poems 1947–1995* (first published in *Howl and Other Poems*, 1956, Penguin Books, 1997). Copyright © Allen Ginsberg, 1956, 1996.

Eamon Grennan – 'To the Moon' by Giacomo Leopardi, translated by Eamon Grennan, by permission of the translator.

Patrick Kavanagh – 'The Hospital' by Patrick Kavanagh, by permission of the Trustees of the Estate of the late Katherine B. Kavanagh, through the Jonathan Williams Literary Agency.

Philip Larkin – 'This Be The Verse' and 'Home is so Sad' by Philip Larkin, by

Index of Poets

Index of Titles

Index of First Lines

Contributors' Biographies

DANNIE ABSE'S *New and Collectged Poems* (2003) was a special commendation of the Poetry Book Society. His most recent poetry volume, *Running Late* (2006), won the Roland Rathias Award.

R. V. BAILEY was born in Northumberland. She acts as a second voice in poetry readings given by U. A. Fanthorpe, and in her poetry audiotapes *Double Act* (Penguin) and *Poetry Quartets* (Bloodaxe). Her publications include *Course Work* (1997), and *Marking Time* (2004).

COLETTE BRYCE has published two poetry collections with Picador, *The Heel of Bernadette* (2000) and *The Full Indian Rope Trick* (2004), and a pamphlet, *The Observations of Aleksandr Svetlov* (2007).

NINA CASSIAN was born in 1924 in Galati, Romania. Her poetry has been published in English in the following collections: *Lady of Miracles* (1983); *Call Yourself Alive: Love Poems* (1988); *Life Sentence* (1990); *Cheerleader for a Funeral* (1992); and *Take My Word For It* (1998).

LINDA CHASE is an American poet who lives in Manchester. Her first collection, *These Goodbyes*, was published by Fatchance Press in 1995. Her two Carcanet Press titles are *The Wedding Spy* (2001) and *Extended Family* (2006). She teaches at MMU, and is the coordinator of the Poetry School Manchester and the director of the reading series, Poets and Players.

GILLIAN CLARKE is president of Ty Newydd, the Writers' Centre in Gwynedd, north Wales, which she co-founded in 1990, and is part-time tutor in doctoral studies in Creative Writing, University of Glamorgan. Recent books include *Collected Poems, Five Fields*, and *Making the Beds for the Dead*, published by Carcanet. She lives in Ceredigion.

BILLY COLLINS is the author of six books of poetry including, most recently, *Nine Horses*. A selection of poems, *Taking Off Emily Dickinson's Clothes*, was published in 2000. Poet Laureate of the United States for 2001–2003, Collins lives with his wife in northern Westchester County, New York.

WENDY COPE was a London primary-school teacher for nearly twenty years. Her first collection of poems, *Making Cocoa for Kingsley Amis*, was published in 1986, and followed by *Serious Concerns* in 1992 and *If I Don't Know* in 2001. She has also written poems for children and edited several anthologies. She is now a freelance writer, living in Winchester.

TONY CURTIS was born in Dublin in 1955. He is the author of seven collections of poetry, the most recent of which, *The Well in the Rain – New & Selected Poems*, was published by Arc in 2006. Curtis has been awarded the Irish National Poetry Prize and is a member of Aosdana, the Irish academy of the arts.

IMTIAZ DHARKER'S cultural experience spans three countries: Pakistan, the country of her birth; Britain, where she grew up; and India, where she spen much of her adult life. She now lives between Bombay, London and Wales. Her books of poems *Purdah*, *Postcards from God*, *I Speak for the Devil* and *The Terrorist At My Table* are all published by Bloodaxe. She is also an artist and a documentary film-maker.

THEO DORGAN is the author of three books of poems: *The Ordinary House of Love*, *Rosa Mundi* and *Sappho's Daughter*. His most recent publications are *Sailing For Home* (2004), *Songs of Earth and Light* (2005) and *A Book of Uncommon Prayer*, edited and compiled by him (2007).

MENNA ELFYN has published ten volumes of poetry, and *Peffaith Nam/Perfect Blemish, New & Selected Poems* will appear in November 2007. She was Poet Laureate for the Children of Wales in 2002. She is a Fellow of the Royal Literary Fund at Swansea University and Writing Director of the MA Creative Writing programme at Trinity College, Carmarthen.

RUTH FAINLIGHT has published thirteen collections of poems, two of short stories and translations of poems from Spanish and Portuguese, and written three opera libretti. Her most recent collection of poems is *Moon Wheels* (2006), and her new translation of Sophocles' Theban Plays, done with Robert Littman, will be published in the USA in 2008 by Johns Hopkins University Press.

U. A. FANTHORPE was born in Kent. Her publications include *Double Act* (1997), *Poetry Quartets 5* (1999), *Christmas Poems* (2003), *Queuing for the Sun* (2003) and *Collected Poems* (2005). She is a Fellow of the Royal Society of Literature, and was appointed CBE in 2001. In 2003 she received the Queen's Gold Medal for Poetry.

JANE FEAVER was born in Durham. She is editor, with Michael Morpurgo, of *Cock Crow: An anthology of poems about the Countryside*. Her novel, *According to Ruth*, is published by Harvill Secker. She lives in Devon with her daughter.

VICKI FEAVER lives in Scotland at the foot of the Pentland Hills. Her third collection of poetry, *The Book of Blood* (2006), was shortlisted for the Forward and Costa prizes.

ELAINE FEINSTEIN has been a Fellow of the Royal Society of Literature since 1980. Her *Collected Poems and Translations* (2002) was a Poetry Book Society Special Commendation. Her biography of Anna Akhmatova, *Anna of All the*

Russias, was published in 2005. Her most recent book of poems is *Talking To The Dead* (2007).

ROY FISHER is the Honorary Poet of the City of Birmingham, where he was born in 1930, and a Fellow of the Royal Society of Literature. Fifty years of his writings are collected in *The Long and the Short of It: Poems 1955–2005* (Bloodaxe).

ROGER GARFITT runs Poetry Masterclasses for the University of Cambridge Institute of Continuing Education at Madingley Hall. His *Selected Poems* are published by Carcanet and he is completing a memoir, *The Horseman's Word*, for Harvill Secker.

DAVID HART holds part-time posts at Warwick and Birmingham universities. He was Birmingham Poet Laureate 1997–98, and has won First and Second in the National Poetry Competition. His books of poetry include *Setting the poem to words*, *Crag Inspector*, *Work, the work* and *Running Out* (2006).

PAUL HENRY is a poet and songwriter from Wales. He has read and performed his work widely, in the UK and in Europe. Since receiving a Gregory Award, he has published four collections of poetry. A fifth, *Ingrid's Husband*, which includes 'The Waiting Room', is due out from Seren this year.

JENNY JOSEPH was born in Birmingham in 1932. She has written prose and poetry for children and adults. *Persephone*, a story in prose and verse, won the James Tait Black Award for fiction in 1986. She has collaborated with photographers, musicians, painters and actors. Her most recent book of poems, *Extreme of things*, was published in 2006.

Poet and playwright LIZ LOCHHEAD was born in Lanarkshire in 1947. From 1986 to 1987 she was the writer in residence at the University of Edinburgh and in 1988 became writer in residence at the Royal Shakespeare Company. She became Glasgow's Poet Laureate in 2005.

ROGER MCGOUGH is a Fellow of the Royal Society of Literature. He is an Honorary Professor of Thames Valley University and a Fellow of John Moores University, Liverpool. He was made a Freeman of the City of Liverpool in 2001, and received a CBE from the Queen in 2004. Currently he presents *Poetry Please* on BBC Radio 4.

IAN MCMILLAN is poet-in-residence for Barnsley FC and the Academy of Urbanism. He is also UK Trade & Investment Poet, C5 News Poet and Humberside Police's Beat Poet. He is a Royal Literary Fund Associate Fellow at Northern College Barnsley, Rotherham College and South Yorkshire WEA.

PAULA MEEHAN has published five collections of poetry, the most recent being *Dharmakaya* (Carcanet), which received the Denis Devlin Memorial Award of the Irish Arts Council. She has also written for the theatre – for both adults and children.

ROBERT MINHINNICK lives in south Wales, where he edits the international quarterly *Poetry Wales*. He has twice won the Forward Prize for Best Individual Poem and twice the Wales Book of the Year for his prose. Carcanet will publish his next collection in summer 2008. 'The Yellow Palm' is based on a visit he made to Baghdad in 1998.

PAUL MULDOON is Howard G. B. Clark '21 Professor at Princeton University and Chair of the University Center for the Creative and Performing Arts. Between 1999 and 2004 he was Professor of Poetry at the University of Oxford. His most recent collections of poetry are *Hay* (1998), *Poems 1968–1998* (2001), *Moy Sand and Gravel* (2002) and *Horse Latitudes* (2006).

SEAN O'BRIEN is Professor of Creative Writing at Newcastle University. He has published six collections of poetry, including, most recently, *The Drowned Book* (2007) and *Downriver* (2001), which won the Forward Prize for Best Collection. His most recent work is *The Drowned Book* (Picador, 2007).

Born in Chicago, JULIE O'CALLAGHAN has lived in Ireland since 1974. Her collections of poetry include *Edible Anecdotes* (1983), *What's What* (1991) and *No Can Do* (2000). Her *New and Selected Poems* will be published by Bloodaxe in 2008. She has received the Michael Hartnett Prize for poetry and is a member of the Irish academy of arts, Aosdána.

Born in Tipperary, Ireland, in 1954, DENNIS O'DRISCOLL's publications include *New & Selected Poems* (2004) and *Troubled Thoughts, Majestic Dreams* (2001), a selection of his essays and reviews. He is editor of The Bloodaxe Book of Poetry Quotations (2006). A new collection, *Reality Check*, is forthcoming.

RUTH PADEL has published six collections (most recently *The Soho Leopard*, shortlisted for the 2004 T. S. Eliot Prize) and won the National Poetry Competition. She is a Fellow of the Royal Society of Literature and her new book on reading poetry, *The Poem and the Journey*, is 'the ideal guide for the apprehensive reader of contemporary poetry' (*Irish Times*).

CRAIG RAINE is Fellow in English at New College, Oxford, and editor of *Areté*. His *Collected Poems 1978–1999* is available from Picador. His critical study *T. S. Eliot* appeared in 2007.

ROBIN ROBERTSON is from the north-east coast of Scotland. His poetry has received various awards, including the Forward Prize for Best First Collection and the E. M. Foster Award. His third collection, *Swithering*, won the 2006 Forward Prize for Best Collection. His book of versions of Tomas Tranströmer's poems, *The Deleted World*, was published in 2006.

CAROL RUMENS is the author of fourteen collections of poems, the latest being *Poems, 1968–2004* (Bloodaxe Books), as well as occasional fiction, drama, and translation. Her prose book, *Self into Song*, was published in 2007. She is currently Professor in Creative Writing at the University of Wales, Bangor, and she is a Fellow of the Royal Society of Literature.

VERNON SCANNELL was born in 1922. He studied for a year at Leeds University and served in the Gordon Highlanders in the Second World War, in North Africa and the D-Day Normandy landings. He has had various jobs including teaching and a spell as a professional boxer.

MICHAEL SCHMIDT is the editorial director of Carcanet Press and editor of the magazine *PN Review*. He is convenor of the Creative Writing M.Litt. at the University of Glasgow where he is Professor of Poetry, and he has published literary history, fiction, and poetry, most recently *The Resurrection of the Body* (Smith/Doorstop).

CLARE SHAW grew up in Burnley, spent ten years in Liverpool and now lives in West Yorkshire. Her first poetry collection, *Straight Ahead*, was published by Bloodaxe in 2006. Clare is also known for her work and publications around women's mental health, and is co-director of harm-ed, a self-harm training partnership.

OWEN SHEERS was born in Fiji in 1974 and brought up in Abergavenny, South Wales. His debut prose work, *The Dust Diaries* (2004), won the Welsh Book of the Year 2005. His second collection of poetry, *Skirrid Hill* (2005), won a Society of Authors Somerset Maugham Award. His first novel, *Resistance* (2007), is published by Faber.

HENRY SHUKMAN's publications include *In Dr No's Garden* (2003), which won the Aldeburgh Poetry Prize, *Sandstorm* (2005), which won the Author's Club First Novel Award, and his second novel, *The Lost City* (2007). His poems have appeared in the *Guardian, The Times, Daily Telegraph, Independent on Sunday, Times Literary Supplement, London Review of Books* and the *New Republic*.

PENELOPE SHUTTLE has lived in Cornwall since 1970 and is the widow of the poet Peter Redgrove (1932–2003). Her eighth collection, *Redgrove's Wife* (2006), was shortlisted for the Forward Prize and for the T. S. Eliot Award. She is a Hawthornden Fellow, and a tutor for the Poetry School, and for the Arvon Foundation. Her daughter Zoe Redgrave is an environmentalist.

JEAN SPRACKLAND's latest book, *Hard Water*, was shortlisted for both the T. S. Eliot Prize and the Whitbread Poetry Award. Her new collection, *Tilt* (2007), is published by Cape.

TOMAS TRANSTRÖMER is generally regarded as Sweden's greatest living poet. In 1990 he suffered a serious stroke which left his speech impaired and his right side paralysed. He lives with his wife in Stockholm and continues to write, and play the piano – a number of pieces for the left hand having been composed specially for him.

JANE WEIR's first collection, *The Way I Dressed During the Revolution* (2005), was shortlisted for the Glen Dimplex New Writers Award 2006. She has also published an audio pamphlet, *Alice* (2006), based partially on the life of Alice Wheeldon. Her two monographs, on Katherine Mansfield and Charlotte Mews, and her second collection, *Before Playing Romeo*, are published in 2007.

JOHN HARTLEY WILLIAMS has published nine collections of poetry, two of which have been shortlisted for the T. S. Eliot Prize. The most recent collection was *Blues* (2004). He is co-author, with Matthew Sweeney, of *Teach Yourself Writing Poetry* (2003). Further prose works include *Ignoble Sentiments* (1995) and *Mystery in Spiderville* (2002). His most recent volume is *The Ship* (2007).

MICHAEL WOODS edits *Tandem* magazine. His poems have appeared in a number of anthologies. He has won prizes in a number of poetry competitions including the Bridport, Ledbury, Poetry on the Lake and Templar. He is the author of *York Notes Advanced* on the poetry of Carol Ann Duffy. He teaches English and Drama at the Chase School in Malvern, Worcestershire.